INFO TASKS

For Successful Learning

Building Skills in Reading, Writing, and Research

Carol Koechlin

Sandi Zwaan

Pembroke Publishers Limited

© 2001 Pembroke Publishers
538 Hood Road
Markham, Ontario, Canada L3R 3K9
www.pembrokepublishers.com

Distributed in the U.S. by Stenhouse Publishers
477 Congress Street
Portland, ME 04101
www.stenhouse.com

We acknowledge the financial support of the Government of Canada through the Book Publishing Industry Development Program (BPIDP) for our publishing activities.

National Library of Canada Cataloguing in Publication Data

Koechlin, Carol
    Info tasks for successful learning: building skills in reading, writing and research

Includes bibliographical references and index.
ISBN 1-55138-133-8

1. Information literacy — Study and teaching (Elementary)
2. Information literacy — Study and teaching (Middle school)
3. Research — Study and teaching (Elementary) 4. Research — Study and teaching (Middle school) 5. Study skills. I. Zwaan, Sandi
II. Title.

ZA3075.K63 2001   371.3   C2001-901393-0

Editor: Jennifer Drope
Cover Design: John Zehethofer
Cover Photo: Ajay Photographics
Typesetting: Jay Tee Graphics Ltd.

Printed and bound in Canada
9 8 7 6 5 4 3 2 1

Table of Contents

Introduction

Info Tasks for Successful Learning is a tool for teachers. It has been designed to help teachers improve student achievement by facilitating student success in information-related tasks.

Measuring student success is frequently the focus of media coverage on educational issues today. Currently it is driving all aspects of the education machine. Our job as teachers is to examine evidence such as assessment results, teaching practices and learning processes, analyze this data, and determine what the results mean and why. After studying the many reports on student performance and investigating to discover the actual areas of weakness, it has become apparent that much of the problem lies with skills related to the processing of information. Whether we look at results in reading and writing or in content areas such as science and history, the evidence points to difficulties with understanding and using information.

Helping students to learn and be successful is the mission we embrace when we enter the teaching profession. Steven Covey in *7 Habits of Highly Effective People* tells us "To begin with the end in mind means to start with a clear understanding of your destination. It means to know where you're going so that you better understand where you are now so that the steps you take are always in the right direction." There is no doubt what our destination is. Parents, students, educators, politicians and business people alike agree. Student success, life-long learning skills and achievement of the expectations set forward in curriculum are our goals. However, getting to our destination has undoubtedly become more complicated.

In recent years, every grade and subject area has been impacted by continuous change. That is natural. Change is what learning is all about. The ability to deal with change is part of being a life-long learner. What is new in curriculum though is not change, but the complexity of the learning experience. New curriculum standards reflect the growing complexity of our global reality.

The rapid emergence of information technologies and the glut of information available to students today introduces many new challenges. Our close investigation of current curriculum standards identified numerous expectations that require sophisticated levels of complex information processing.

In the context of this book we hope to unravel for teachers a segment of teaching and learning that has always been important, but is rapidly being recognized as not only important but key to student success in all areas of the curriculum. In today's information-rich environment, information processing is a vital component of the worlds of work and play.

- Are we giving sufficient thought to the implications the real world holds for education?
- Are we equipping our students with the skills they will need to be successful citizens?
- Are we providing students with relevant real-world learning experiences?
- Are we teaching information literacy skills?

Today's students live in a world where increases in the amount of information being produced will continue to be exponential. Rapid change will undoubtedly be the norm in their world. All we know about their future in this millennium is that these young citizens of tomorrow will need to be ready for a strobe-like environment. They must be able to deal with change at a rapid pace. They need to be savvy users of information. They need to know how information works and how information can work for them.

Info Tasks can help. *Info Tasks,* applied to its full potential, offers teachers the opportunity to help their students become information literate by:

✔ assisting teachers in helping students to deal more effectively with information
✔ providing teachers with strategies and techniques for nudging students to higher levels of achievement
✔ providing strategies for skills that are transferable to many subjects and situations
✔ helping teachers be more reflective about teaching and learning

---

Facilitating Success in Information Processing

To facilitate student success in information processing, we need to question whether our students are well equipped with a "life-support system" of learning skills. For example:

• Can our students define their information needs and develop meaningful and probing questions?
• Do they have knowledge of places and ways to explore their information needs in order to gather the very best resources?
• Can they analyze the relevance and authenticity of the data they collect?
• Are they able to examine data from various perspectives, deconstruct it, look at it with new eyes and ultimately form their own personal opinions?
• Do our students have the ability to see relationships, make connections and transfer their learning to new and innovative situations?
• Do our students have the learning, unlearning and relearning skills they will need to function in their new world?

Most importantly though, we need to ask — what do we want to happen when children work with information? If all we want is a simple recalling of facts, then an assignment asking students to learn "all about" something is adequate. In this case, regurgitation of data discovered, along with a few graphics, will suffice. If we ask them to explore opinions as well, students will most likely investigate and reword the ideas of others. But is that really all we want?

Don't we want students to go beyond collecting data and spouting it back in a slightly different and likely inferior manner? If so, we need to design assignments that will avoid the "cut, paste and plagiarize" approach to research. Surely we want our students to see relevance, to make personal connections and to gain knowledge and understanding. This means we need to design assignments that require students to analyze and synthesize and reflect on their findings. They need to transfer their learning to new and different situations and to share and apply new knowledge. This process will allow students to make connections to real life. It will make the learning experience meaningful, relevant and also more interesting. Students will be learning not only to "do school," but also to "do life."

To assist students in moving to a higher level in their processing of information, we need to ensure that they are information-literate, life-long learners who possess a variety of skills. Specifically, they need to be able to:

✔ Locate information quickly and efficiently
✔ Use a variety of information-gathering strategies
✔ Locate relevant information from a variety of sources
✔ Select what is useful and current
✔ Select only the data they need from all the available sources
✔ Process and record selected data efficiently
✔ Understand form and format of information
✔ Analyze and synthesize information
✔ Share what they have learned through a variety of oral, written and multimedia presentations
✔ Engage in literary and media experiences
✔ Honor the work of others by using appropriate referencing and citation
✔ Demonstrate their learning so that others can learn from them
✔ Apply what they have learned to new and different situations
✔ Optimize the use of technology to enhance their learning
✔ Evaluate their own learning processes and set goals for their improvement

> How can we design learning experiences to facilitate achievement of these skills? First, we must believe in our students' abilities to achieve personal levels of excellence. Second, we must cultivate the same belief in our own abilities as facilitators of excellence in learning experiences. Third, we must approach the preparation of teaching and learning experiences as a design process that starts with student understanding as the desired result. And finally, we must overtly teach our students information processing skills so they can attain understanding and consequently improve their assessment results.

Many ask — how do we, as teachers, design and evaluate these effective and engaging information tasks? There are many research and inquiry models that lay out all stages of the research process. To help teachers think about what they need to do at each stage of the design process for information tasks, we have prepared a tool entitled *Information Task Design Process,* found on page 8. *Designing the Stages of an Info Task*, on page 9, shows how processing information fits into the larger picture of "doing research." The *Information Literacy Rubric* provided on page 10 illustrates how a teacher might assess a student at all stages of the research process, including information processing.

Information Task Design Process

Identify desired results

Just what is it that I want my students to know, understand and be able to do?

How can I cluster and prioritize the learning expectations to peak student interest and ensure student understanding?

Collaborate with the teacher librarian to identify the information processing expectations required for the task.

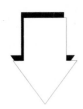

Determine acceptable evidence

How will I know when students have achieved the desired results?

What will I accept as evidence of student understanding and proficiency?

How will I collect evidence over the course of the information task?

How will I provide feedback to students throughout the task?

Design a culminating task that clearly allows students to demonstrate their achievement of the key expectations.
Establish criteria and achievement levels directly linked to the information and topic/subject expectations.
Measure both the process and the performance.

Plan learning experiences and instruction

What do I need to consider at each stage of the project process, to ensure that my students are ultimately able to construct knowledge and understanding?

What activities will help students build the needed knowledge and skills?

How can I make the stages/steps effectively build on each other?

What prerequisite skills need to be in place or reviewed?

What will need to be taught or facilitated in light of the desired learning?

What resources, materials and technologies are needed?

What student groupings are best for each teaching and learning strategy?

What modifications do I need to make for special needs students?

(Based on "The Backward Design Process" in *Understanding by Design* by Wiggins and McTighe)

Designing the Stages of an Info Task

Prepare
❑ How will I provide sufficient, informative exploration of the topic so students will have a working knowledge of the topic before they begin their investigation?
❑ What activities will help students define and clarify their information needs?
❑ How will I know when students are ready to proceed?
❑ How can I make sure that students understand the parameters of the task? (e.g., assessment criteria, timelines, presentation format, etc.)

Access
❑ Where will students access the necessary data?
❑ What are the best sources for this kind of information? Primary, secondary or both?
❑ How will they gather the information?
❑ Do students have prerequisite selection and retrieval skills?
❑ How will students keep track of their information sources?
❑ How can I make sure that students have used a variety of resources?

Process
❑ How can I help students evaluate resources for validity and usefulness?
❑ How can I help students analyze their gathered data?
❑ What strategies would help students sort their data and look for trends and relationships?
❑ How can I help students sort out facts and opinions?
❑ What strategies will help students discover cause and effect?
❑ How can I make sure students have explored their issue from multiple perspectives?
❑ How can I help students synthesize their information and make personal meaning?
❑ How can I help students to make judgments, form opinions and draw conclusions?
❑ What activities would help students to discover the potential consequences or the impact of their discoveries?

Transfer
❑ What strategies would give students opportunities to defend their point of view?
❑ How can I give students authentic opportunities to share their new learning with others?
❑ How can I ensure that students make use of or apply their new learning?
❑ What strategies might help students discover the relevance and importance of their learning?
❑ How can I help students identify their strengths and weaknesses and set goals for personal improvement?

(Based on the four stages of Inquiry/Research in *Information Studies Kindergarten to Grade 12,* OSLA, 1999)

Information Literacy Rubric

	1	2	3	4
Prepare for Research	• Uses a few resources to gain an overview • Defines a need which results in fact gathering	• Uses a variety of resources to gain an overview • Defines a need which produces retelling	• Explores a wide range of resources to build a knowledge base • Defines a need which stimulates a quest for personal meaning	• Explores a wide range of resources and perspectives as well as connections to prior learning to build a knowledge base • Defines a need which evokes original insight and invention
Access Resources	• Locates resources related to the topic • Needs assistance to use search tools	• Selects a variety of relevant resources • Uses table of contents, indexes and bookmarked Internet sites to find information	• Uses search strategies to select a variety of relevant resources • Uses keywords and appropriate search engines to seek required information	• Uses search strategies and evaluation criteria to select a variety of the best resources to meet defined need • Understands how information is organized and readily finds information needed in both print and electronic format, utilizing appropriate search tools
Process Information	• Sorts data • Restates information	• Orders and ranks data • Summarizes information in response to defined need	• Classifies data and makes comparisons • Regroups information, draws conclusions and forms opinions	• Experiments with imaginative reorganization of data • Regroups information, and creates original structures and new ideas based on analysis
Transfer Learning	• Shares limited information • Identifies new learning	• Presents some meaningful information • Identifies new learning and reflects on uses	• Communicates personal learning effectively • Relates new learning to personal experience and information need	• Facilitates new learning for others • Uses knowledge in new situations
Information Technology	• Uses technologies to access information	• Uses technologies to access and record information	• Selects appropriate technologies to access, record and present information	• Integrates technologies, where appropriate to interpret and communicate information
Legal and Ethical Use of Information	• Is aware of copyright ©	• Acknowledges the work of others	• Understands copyright (and references sources appropriately)	• Respects and follows copyright © and acquires permission, where necessary

Using This Book

Data is a collection of raw facts. The process of organizing and analyzing data produces **Information**. The process of synthesizing this information and using one's own ideas to create something new leads to **Knowledge** and **Wisdom**.

(*Teaching Tools for the Information Age*, Koechlin/Zwaan, 1997)

Info Tasks will work with whichever model you choose to teach information skills. In this book, we have concentrated our work not on the overall design of formal research projects, but on the vital stage that we often find is missing or underdeveloped — processing skills related to information. In this stage, students begin with data and end with personal knowledge.

All stages of the research process are equally important to the task as a whole but without the processing stage it is very difficult for students to gain any personal understanding of an issue or content. Without processing skills students achieve only physical access to information. It is when students develop and use discrete processing skills that they gain intellectual access to information. Only then do they have the capacity to achieve real understanding and develop personal knowledge.

We have repeatedly been asked for assistance in designing learning experiences at the processing stage of research. *Info Tasks* explicitly addresses this stage and the complex skills within it. We have clustered the many explicit micro skills inherent in information processing into four macro skills. These include:

- Evaluating Information for Relevance and Validity
- Sorting Information to Make Connections
- Working with Information and Testing Ideas
- Analyzing and Synthesizing Findings and Drawing Conclusions

These macro skills are often taught and assessed as single skills. Although useful for classifying similar processes, they are really much too big and complex to treat as single skills. It is at the micro skill level that we need to teach and assess, as we will demonstrate in the info tasks throughout this book.

Although each chapter of *Info Tasks* is organized around a macro skill, each task is designed to address a micro skill — complete with the desired student learning, an explanation of the task, suggested teaching and learning strategies and a demonstration of that understanding.

Information tasks require that students know how to process data and ideas to create personal understanding. To enable students to effectively and efficiently develop these skills, teachers need to spiral the introduction and development of the many complex skills involved. The macro skills illustrated in the diagram on the next page are only achievable if students are taught the many micro skills embedded in each. These micro skills are specific and precise. They can be taught, practised, observed and assessed. The macro skills are broad general skills and useful to cluster the micro skills into processing categories. To be successful, each micro skill needs to be introduced and developed in the context of relevant curriculum content.

Building Information Processing Capacity
— during the Processing Stage of information tasks

Celebrate and share new learning

Analyzing and synthesizing
findings and drawing conclusions

Working with information
and testing ideas

Sorting information
to make connections

Evaluating information
for relevance and validity

Define information need

Students need to be taught how to be more cognizant of the skills they are learning and their impact on the learning process. Eventually students should take more responsibility for appropriately transferring those critical skills to information problems. As we are designing learning experiences to help students learn and practise these skills, we need to keep in mind the power of having students work collaboratively and the use of graphic organizers and reflective prompts to help students gain capacity to process information. Students also need opportunities to learn about the potential that information technologies offer to make their work more effective and efficient.

Many of the strategies we have suggested in the *Info Task* activities are not new to teachers. They are for the most part tried-and-true ideas with a different twist. The difference is in the way we have sought out what we feel is the best approach or the best use of strategies to help students build specific information skills and understanding of the content area, simultaneously and seamlessly. We want to encourage teachers to be more deliberate about matching learning strategies, task assessment tools and resources to the desired student learning.

In this book, we have also attempted to help teachers learn how to be more reflective about the teaching process. We hope that the many reflective questions and prompts that we offer in *Info Tasks* will help you to continuously and naturally approach teaching as an inquiry.

We urge teachers to approach the design of teaching and learning experiences methodically. Do a little elbow thinking as the students work. Start jotting down reactions and observations. Begin asking yourself probing questions about what you are doing and why. You might ask:

- How do students receive my assignments?
- How well are my students performing?
- How well are my strategies working? Why?
- How can I improve results?
- How can I reuse and reinforce things that are working well?

We also wish to encourage teachers during the teaching process to teach students how to take ownership of their own learning. We need to provide continuous feedback for students so they can set goals for improvement. They need a repertoire of skills and strategies and they need to experiment to discover which ones are most effective and efficient for each information task. Again, the process should be very deliberate for students. They need to think about and develop an understanding of how they learn. Eventually they will be more engaged in "doing school" for themselves, rather than for their teacher. It is at this point that they will be well on the way to becoming life-long learners.

We suggest that you begin to build a repertoire of strategies to use to help students process information critically and creatively. Looking at expectations in the content areas of each subject to discover where information processing skills are required is a good starting point.

The more than 50 tasks in this book can help too. Although the lessons are often set within a specific curriculum content area, they are very generic and can be adapted to many other topics as well. They are also representative of skills needed from primary to senior grades, even though they are not arranged chronologically. Every task we have included can be adapted up or down to address the needs of different ages and abilities.

These are not detailed tasks, but simply ideas to facilitate skill building and enable learners to reach higher levels of understanding and consequently higher levels of achievement. Each one focuses on a particular information-processing skill. These ideas do not necessarily represent the full complement of information-processing skills students need. The micro skills we selected are the ones found over and over again in our review of curriculum standards. The terms are commonly embedded in student expectations/outcomes and are often assumed or lost in the focus on content. These information-processing skills are critical in helping students to construct meaning.

Some skills are very dependent on others. We have tried to arrange the tasks in a continuum within each macro skill-based chapter. For instance, before students can make comparisons, they must be able to identify key facts and ideas, cluster the points and look for similarities and differences.

We need to deliberately construct the learning experience so that each activity builds on the next. Think of it like creating a delicious trifle. You can't toss raspberries, eggs, milk, sugar, peaches and cream into a bowl and expect it to magically become a grand dessert. It doesn't matter how beautiful the bowl is either. You will not end up with the desired outcome unless you carefully and deliberately prepare and process each layer of the

Reflect

review

rethink

revisit

rework

redesign

revise …

trifle. Carefully layering each component allows you to build your sumptuous creation.

Experiment with the *Info Tasks* strategies and ideas offered. Adapt them to meet the needs of your students. When you are designing research assignments and projects like WebQuests, consider using *Information Task Design Process* on page 8 to help you think about the critical elements in all information tasks. Pay particular attention to building capacity for success at the processing stage. Examine the learning expectations/standards from content curriculum carefully. Look for those macro skills and break them down into teachable micro skills. Use and adapt the micro skill strategies that are found in each task offered in the following chapters to help your students build a repertoire of information skills they can transfer to other situations.

The goal in the end is to help your students capture the excitement of working with information. The results will be improved reading, writing and research skills achievement. Design your lessons with student success in mind.

CHAPTER ONE

Evaluating Information for Relevance and Validity

Once students have gathered resources, they are ready to select, process and record data that is relevant to their needs. They need to organize the data they have selected and record their sources. They also need to evaluate their information according to several criteria— such as relevance and validity. The tasks in this chapter address many facets of data evaluation.

Not all information is factual. The advent of the Internet as an information source has heightened the need for students to acquire and effectively apply validation skills. Anyone can post anything on the Internet, making it difficult to confirm the credibility of some sites. All information needs to be closely examined for evidence of bias and propaganda. Students also need to consider the currency of information regarding such topics as population.

In the course of evaluating information, we must all be diligent about respecting copyright. The advent of electronic data and word processing programs has increased the potential for plagiarism unless information tasks are carefully designed. The quantity and quality of data collected must continuously be assessed.

The tasks that follow assist students in becoming critical users of information by allowing them to:

- Locate, survey or interview to collect data
- Determine which data is relevant to their current need(s)
- Identify and separate fact from opinion
- Discover explicit bias and understand the impact it has on the value of the information
- Detect inconsistencies among data from different sources
- Assess the data collected to ensure that they have everything necessary
- Be aware of the ethical and legal implications of using digital information

Identifying Relevant Resources

Clarifying the Task

This task provides an interesting subject — endangered species — for students to discover the quantity and range of information available on a given topic. It also provides an opportunity for students to apply their search and selection skills as they identify the best resources available, and then identify within those resources the information required for their inquiry.

Building Understanding

Introduce the topic by reading and discussing a picture book that deals with endangered species.

Divide students into groups and assign each group a different continent to explore. Explain that the students will need to research resources for their continent in order to investigate threatened and endangered species. Book time in the school library and ask the teacher librarian to review search strategies with your students. Ask each group to brainstorm and record places they could search for information. Have students divide up the possible sources and assign everyone in the group specific responsibilities. Remind students about criteria for successful group work.

Tell students that they will not be reading their information sources closely at this point. Explain that they will be skimming and scanning to get an overview and validate the sources as being accurate and authentic. Inform students that they will locate and select the best sources (e.g., reference books, magazines, Internet, CD-ROM, newspapers, pamphlets, posters, etc.) on the topic for their continent. Ask them to bring their best sources back to their tables.

Provide each group with a large table, display board(s), book stands, colored paper and markers. Have students display the best resources they discovered for the threatened and endangered species on the continent they were assigned. Remind students that each member of their group needs to be conversant with the material at their kiosk because they will each take a turn being the curator at their display.

Demonstrating Understanding

Provide each student with a booklet that resembles a passport. Instruct students to travel to every information kiosk to identify and record a defined number of threatened and endangered species for each continent. Encourage students to record those species that they are really curious about because they will be selecting one of these for further investigation. Leave the information kiosks up in the school library or another convenient location so students can continue to access the selected resources for their research.

Determining Relevant Data

Info Task

Students work with text to determine what is relevant to their information needs.

Clarifying the Task

Selecting the data students need from text is a very difficult task. Most of the processing requires students to constantly refer to their defined need to decide which data to eliminate and which to keep. This process should be modeled, but students must apply it in the context of an information problem they are working on for them to take ownership of the skill. This strategy can be applied to simply making notes from a text or to undertaking a far more complex research task.

Building Understanding

Ask students to come to this activity well organized with some sort of information problem in mind. Ensure that their information problem — inquiry question, focus for research, hypothesis or teacher-directed question — is in print so that they can continually refer back to it. Give students a few minutes to articulate to a partner what information they are looking for.

Before students begin to examine an information source or sources, review these prompts for determining relevance:

> - Which data answers my question, problem or focus?
> - What is repetitive?
> - What is supporting evidence?
> - What is not needed?
> - What is interesting but not needed for this task?
> - Which information is factual?
> - Which information represents someone's opinion?
> - Which information do I disagree with? Why?

Have students refer to these thinking prompts as they select relevant information from the text. Ask them to record the information they select in point form by applying note-taking skills.

Instruct the students to continue using their information source(s) until they have enough data to begin working on their information problem.

Demonstrating Understanding

Have students work with a partner using the prompts from the Info Task *Identifying Missing Information* on page 21 to determine if their recorded data is relevant, and to examine the quality and quantity of what they have recorded.

Check It Out

Your students may need assistance to refine basic note-taking skills and strategies. To effectively process information they need to be able to make point-form notes, create outlines and do information mapping.

Determining Fact and Opinion

Clarifying the Task

Students are often required to write opinion pieces as a demonstration of their understanding. Before students can effectively develop their own opinions and write about them, they need to deconstruct some information texts such as magazine and newspaper articles in order to be able to recognize and differentiate between fact and opinion in such texts.

Building Understanding

Using an overhead and colored pens, show students examples of facts and opinions from selected texts.

Brainstorm characteristics of *fact* and *opinion* based on these examples. Characteristics may include:

> *Facts*
>
> - Events that actually occurred
> - Information that is exact and provable
> - Information that is specific and accurate
>
> *Opinions*
>
> - Views, thoughts, feelings and judgments
> - Conclusions that may be unproven
> - Words and phrases such as virtually, clearly, no doubt, most, almost none, it is apparent, etc.
> - Data that is not supported by facts

Source and obtain permission to copy a short article such as an editorial from a weekly newsmagazine. Ask students to read the article and identify points that appear to be factual as well as those that they believe to be the opinion of the author. Remind students to look for trigger words as clues to opinions. Where necessary, have students check "facts" for validity.

Demonstrating Understanding

Instruct students to record their discoveries using the *Linking to Facts and Opinions* organizer on page 83. This organizer prompts students to make personal connections to information as they analyze it.

Check It Out

Give students opportunities to practise the skill of distinguishing between fact and opinion using video, Internet sites, textbooks and pamphlets.

Discovering Bias

Info Task
Students examine current print media for evidence of explicit biases.

Clarifying the Task

It is critical for students to be able to analyze information for explicit biases. They will need to transfer this skill to many tasks such as evaluating information for a research report, making a major purchase or participating in a discussion or debate. The following set of activities is designed to engage students in active identification and classification of types of biases.

Building Understanding

Begin by reviewing/introducing major forms of bias. Familiarize students with trigger words they should watch for. For example:

- Exaggerations — *The greatest ...*
- Charged words — *... voluntary implementation ...*
- Overgeneralizations — *... all people who ...*
- Opinions asserted as facts — *... it is well known that ...*
- Inclusions/exclusions — *... the only view to consider ...*
- Prejudices — *My ... I ...We ...*

Group students and give each group one form of bias as its focus. Give each group a selection of newspapers, magazines, commercial flyers and pamphlets. Provide a range of resources that will offer a broad spectrum of biases. Instruct students to skim through these texts and look for evidence of the specific form of bias they are responsible for. Also, guide students to look for a range of evidence (e.g., examples dealing with age, gender, culture and socio-economic conditions). Ask students to clip out the examples they discover and continue searching. Encourage students to share other forms of bias they discover with appropriate groups.

Afterward, have the students arrange their evidence in an interesting collage that they should mount and label. Have them prepare to share their findings. If students have not had previous experience in detecting bias you will need to do more teaching and modeling.

Demonstrating Understanding

Display the finished collages. Encourage students to be on the alert for bias and to continue to add to the display (clipping only with permission). Keep the dialogue going with your class by asking students questions such as:

- Have you discovered biases you were not aware of previously?
- Were you surprised by how much/little you discovered?
- Are you able to make any relationships between what you found and where you found it?
- Why is it important to be aware of bias?

Check It Out
Sometimes it is easier to see bias if you have something else with which to compare it. Provide students with several articles or infomercials on the same topic and have students analyze them for bias.

Detecting Inconsistencies

Info Task
Students analyze information for accuracy by comparing two media items or texts and looking for inconsistencies.

Clarifying the Task

Students are often hindered by the glut of information they discover. They need to know how to validate information to make sure it is accurate and authentic. In this task students will gain skills for validating sources by detecting inconsistencies and analyzing the reasons for the variations.

Building Understanding

Arrange students into groups of three or four. Give each group two sets of text or media. For example, select a news story from two different newspapers, a topic in history from two different textbooks, or two videos of relatively the same length on the same topic. Invite students to actively interact with the text as they read, view and/or listen.

Tell the students that their role in this exercise is to discover inconsistencies/contradictions by comparing the two bodies of information. Explain that they will need to look for things like inconsistent numbers, dates, places and names, as well as forms of bias. Instruct students to individually record their evidence on adhesive notes or a chart as they discover it. If the text is photocopied, have students highlight evidence. Invite the students to share their inconsistencies and confirm their discoveries with the group.

Once students have examined their information sources, have them record their findings on the *Detecting Inconsistencies* organizer on page 84 and then discuss and record possible reasons for the inconsistencies. If your students have not had experience working with information to detect bias and distinguish between facts and opinions, see Info Tasks *Discovering Bias* and *Determining Fact and Opinion* on pages 19 and 18.

Demonstrating Understanding

Book time with the teacher librarian to assist students in searching for more resources on the same topic (e.g., books, on-line databases, Internet sites, videos, etc.). Instruct students to search for information to validate or refute the information in question.

Afterward, ask the students to complete a reflection about the process they have followed and the implications this has for future information processing. Following are some sample prompts:

> • What strategies did you use to compare your information?
> • What did you find out about the accuracy of information?
> • What surprised you the most?
> • What do these discoveries mean for your future quests for accurate information?
> • How will these discoveries affect your reactions to media or text in the future?

Check It Out
For more help with validating sources see *Information Power Pack Junior/Intermediate Skillsbooks* (Koechlin and Zwaan, 1997).

Identifying Missing Information

Info Task
Students identify areas where information is missing and devise an action plan for filling the gaps, once they have analyzed data for relevance and adequacy for their information need.

Clarifying the Task

In this task students practise thinking strategies which they can apply to any information task to ensure that they have enough quality information.

Building Understanding

When students have spent some time on data collection for a research project they need to STOP and think about the quantity and quality of the data they have collected. This is an excellent time to schedule some peer conferencing sessions.

Ask students to make an appointment with a peer to meet at a designated conferencing area in your classroom or library. Instruct students to look at each other's data through critical lenses. Provide students with the following "data check" prompts so they have the necessary criteria to assist each other with improving their data collection.

> • Do you have enough data to address your inquiry question?
> • Is all the data on topic?
> • Are you excited about what you have discovered?
> • What perspectives have been included?
> • Whose voice is missing?
> • Do you have any conflicting data?
> • Do you see any trends or patterns?
> • What have you learned?
> • What do you still need to find out?
> • Where will you look next for needed data?

Demonstrating Understanding

Ask all students to summarize their progress to date on a memo pad or large adhesive pad and list "to do" items so that they can be checked off as they are accomplished. The teacher/teacher librarian will need to scan these notes, conference with students and offer assistance where needed to help students fill in any gaps in their information.

Check It Out

Remind students to keep all their source sheets, printouts, organizers and assignment notes together in a research folder.

Analyzing Implications

Info Task
Students analyze the legal and ethical implications of using digital information.

Clarifying the Task

Students need to be aware of the legal and ethical issues surrounding digital information and what the implications are for accessing, using and posting information. In this task the students explore the broad spectrum of issues associated with digital information and analyze the implications for them as users.

Building Understanding

Organize students into small groups to discuss:

- What is digital information?
- How do we use digital information?
- How is it misused?

Afterward, have one student in each group act as the recorder to create a chart of the group's responses. Share and discuss the group responses and post in the classroom for future reference.

Explain to the students that they will be investigating the issues surrounding the use of digital information in order to create a "cybertips campaign" to inform fellow students and make them aware of the implications for students and other users.

Invite your students and your teacher librarian to help create a collection of resources that will be available for all students to use in their investigations. Include items such as the school code of conduct and school/board Internet policy, as well as articles, videos and Web sites dealing with copyright laws, rules, regulations and conventions, plagiarism, nettiquette, cyberstalkers, hackers, net safety, viruses, etc.

Allow students time to skim and scan these materials to identify as many issues as possible. Have students work in pairs on their analysis of issues related to the use of digital information. Ask them to identify and analyze at least one issue related to ethics, conventions and copyright, using a chart similar to the one below. Remind students to consider positive and negative implications, as well as all the parties involved.

	Accessing	Using	Posting	Implications (who)
Ethics				
Conventions				
Copyright				

Demonstrating Understanding

Have students embark on an information campaign to inform other students of the issues and implications involved in using digital information. Ask them to select an area from their analysis to focus on for the campaign. Have students brainstorm ways they could get their message out to the student body (e.g., posters for the hall of the school, ads on the public address system, pages for the school Web site, etc.) As a group, establish a format and criteria for creating and presenting the cybertips. Explain that the ultimate goal of this exercise is to help students become aware of the implications of using digital information and to become personally responsible.

Check It Out
Use a similar process to have students discover the legal and ethical issues and the implications pertaining to music, video and traditional print.

CHAPTER TWO

Sorting Information to Make Connections

Once students have made interesting discoveries, gathered their data and recorded it on organizers, they must begin the process that takes them beyond physical access. As students begin to work with data and organize it to make meaningful information, they require a working knowledge of a variety of skills. They need opportunities to manipulate, reorganize, regroup, sort, categorize, classify and cluster data so that they can begin to see connections and make relationships. The tasks in this chapter depend on the students' ability to apply and, if necessary, develop the skills of fluency and flexibility.

Initially the teacher will need to provide students with organizers for sorting information, but eventually students will use computer software to create their own. When students use graphic organizers to sort their data into sub-topics, they are beginning to set up for more complex analysis. Sorting skills are prerequisite for higher-level analysis.

The tasks that follow offer opportunities for students to:

- Identify and record key points
- Select information and order it by ranking, sequencing, classifying and clustering
- Order and reorder information using different categories and criteria
- Identify two or more bodies of information and compare the details
- Recognize similarities and differences as they compare
- Identify relationships and make connections
- Compare kinds of data from different sources to determine which sources are best for specific needs

Identifying Key Points

Info Task
Students locate relevant information from a variety of sources, and identify and record key points.

Clarifying the Task

Students need to have a series of strategies for identifying key points and recording those points modeled for them. Afterward, students require many opportunities to practise these skills so they can develop a personal process that works well for them. During this task students will observe and try out many strategies that they can use to identify and record key points in an information source or sources.

Building Understanding

Before students begin to gather information on a topic, ask yourself:

- Have students had sufficient opportunity to explore the topic being studied?
- Have they developed good inquiry questions, sub-topics and keywords to help with searches?
- Can they employ active reading, viewing and listening skills?

Identifying, selecting and recording key points happen almost simultaneously as students collect the most relevant sources and determine the most relevant data. To help students select key points, provide them with a list of criteria similar to the following:

- Relevant to your focus
- Accurate
- Current
- Interesting
- Inclusive
- Valid

After the defined needs are established, try modeling some strategies for identifying key points using:

- A data projector or overhead projector for highlighting important words.
- Photocopies or printouts of a selected text so that students can learn how to highlight key points using a different-colored highlighter for each sub-topic.
- Adhesive notes so that students can use these as placeholders for key ideas as they scan texts or to record their own big ideas and questions as they interact with text.
- Point-form note taking to record selected ideas on organizers.
- Index cards for recording relevant points from one source on each card, where each point begins with a nugget.
- A computer to demonstrate features of notepads and word processing.

Demonstrating Understanding

Before students continue with an information task they need to do a quality check on the key points they have identified. See Info Tasks *Determining Relevant Data* and *Identifying Missing Information* on pages 17 and 21 for ideas on how to assess the quality of data.

Check It Out
Using the organizer *Working with Information* on page 85, try some strategies to help students work with information as they are recording key points.

Sequencing

Clarifying the Task

This task requires students to collect, sort and sequence information about someone who is important to them. Begin by making connections to other sequencing activities the students have done.

Building Understanding

Review the concept of change over time and chart changes using an example such as plant growth.

Afterward, read *Love You Forever* by Robert Munsch or a similar story dealing with change over time. Discuss feelings from the perspective of different characters. In the case of *Love You Forever,* this includes the boy, the mother, and the listener. Discussion questions might include:

- Who was important to the mother?
- How did the boy change over time?
- How did the mother change?

Chart changes that are identified. Assign a year of a character's (e.g., the boy) life to each student. Instruct students to draw (on a card) an illustration that relates what the character was like at that age. As they peg their cards to a clothesline chronologically, ask students to tell about the character at that time in his/her life. When the line is complete it becomes a collective time line. Invite students to retell the story from the clothesline of picture cards.

Demonstrating Understanding

Discuss people who are important to students at school and at home. Instruct students to choose a person who is important to them, to question that person, and to record on a copy of a sheet like the *Important Person Survey* shown below a number of significant changes that have occurred during that person's lifetime.

Important Person Survey

My important person is _____

_____ is important because _____

When _____ was a baby _____

When _____ went to school_____

Most important events

- _____
- _____
- _____
- _____

Today _____ is _____

Back in class, ask the students to create illustration cards and to make a pictorial timeline for their important person. Invite them to share their timeline stories with other students. Conference with the students to determine if they are able to explain why a person is important to them and if they can sequence the changes they have identified in chronological order.

Classifying

Info Task

Students rely on their observations to classify rocks and minerals according to specified criteria.

Check It Out

Read *The Magic Pebble* by William Steig. Discuss fictional and real uses for rocks. Have each student select one rock from the classroom collection. Instruct them to brainstorm and record words and phrases that describe their rock and potential uses it could have. Invite your students to plan and draft a short story about their rock using descriptive words and phrases from their brainstormed list. Share stories orally in small groups.

Clarifying the Task

Students are often instructed to classify information. Experiences with sorting and identifying criteria are prerequisites for classifying. In this task students experience these skills through a tactile learning experience, which they can then transfer to other less concrete information classification tasks.

Building Understanding

As part of a study of rocks and minerals, gather samples and bring them to school and/or ask students to bring them in. These can be found samples or commercially available samples. Develop some guidelines for rock collecting if students are going to collect their own samples.

Working in small groups, instruct students to discuss how their samples are alike and different. Ensure that your students have had sufficient exploratory activities to provide them with a working vocabulary and adequate knowledge about rocks for this activity.

In the large group, share suggestions for criteria (e.g., color, texture, size, dull, shiny, etc.). As a class, decide on 8 to 10 critical criteria for classifying rocks and minerals. Once these are agreed upon, prepare a large cross-classification chart for the floor or a tabletop. The chart will look something like this:

Texture / Appearance	smooth	rough	jagged	bumpy
dull				
shiny				
speckled				
layered				

Have students work in pairs to classify a number of rocks, placing them in the appropriate sections on the chart. Ask students to articulate their reasons for the categories they selected.

Demonstrating Understanding

When everyone has classified a number of rocks, hold a sharing circle to discuss observations, questions they have, and any new criteria they have thought of. Talk about classifications that were challenging and ask students to suggest ways to confirm their choices (e.g., field guides, reference books, etc.).

Clustering

Clarifying the Task

Food packaging is an information source that students need to learn to interpret. In this task students examine packaging text to find specific information about food value. Based on the information on the packaging, students look for similarities and form clusters. This task would be most successfully done while working on a nutrition unit when students have a background knowledge of food nutrients and their importance for healthy living.

Building Understanding

Ask students to collect empty, clean food packages and bring a variety of containers to class. Limitations need to be established around safety issues like food allergies and breakable containers.

Provide large surfaces for the students to work on. Divide students into groups and make sure that each group has a variety of packages with which to work. Ask students to read labels and record information that is relevant to nutritional value. They could use adhesive notes, charts, or work with a simple database. Have students also note promotional information and claims that they discover on the packaging.

Explain to students that you want them to look for similarities among the products and to cluster them into groups that have similar characteristics. Encourage students to apply knowledge they may have gained from a nutrition unit. In groups, have students find similarities and discuss possible groupings (e.g., carbohydrates, fats, proteins, vitamins, minerals, levels within one nutrient — such as level of sugar content, etc.).

Have the groups cluster their packages and prepare to report on their clustering criteria, as well as how and why they chose the criteria. Ask them also to report on any discrepancies or questions/concerns they may have around promotional information found on the packaging.

Demonstrating Understanding

After sharing their observations with the class, ask students to individually write a learning summary and reflection regarding their discoveries about food packaging and what the implications are for them personally and for their community. To extend the learning, have students re-examine their criteria, develop different criteria and cluster again.

Check It Out

This task offers opportunities to discuss packaging in general and how it relates to our environment. Visit some of the many Web sites with nutrition information related to packaging. Try the following keywords: nutrition, labeling, education.

Recognizing Similarities and Differences

Info Task

Students make comparisons by recognizing similarities and differences between features of a medieval home and a home of the 2000s.

Similar	Different

Check It Out

Ask the teacher librarian to help you select a good variety of well illustrated medieval picture books for the students to use. For ideas on teaching children to read pictures, consult a resource such as *Teaching Tools for the Information Age* (Koechlin and Zwaan, 1997).

Clarifying the Task

In this task, students begin by building background knowledge about the features of their own homes and how they are similar and different. As much of the reading material on Medieval Times is written at a high reading level, we suggest that you teach students how to read pictures and other visuals for information on medieval homes. In this way, students will be challenged to think a little deeper about their findings and to speculate why homes were different in Medieval Times.

Building Understanding

Ask students to draw a picture of a room in their home. Later, go on a walk in the school community with students and take photographs or video footage of different kinds of homes. Introduce the terms similar and different. Ask students to find similarities among the homes in their community. Chart these. Ask students to look for major differences. Chart these as well.

Take your class to the school library and work with the teacher librarian to help students find a variety of visual resources on medieval homes (e.g., picture books, fact books, charts and videos). Ensure that the students are discovering resources that are representative of a diversity of world cultures in Medieval Times.

Remind students to be active readers, viewers and listeners as they explore the resources. Instruct students to pay close attention in particular to pictures, drawings and charts. As students are working, ask them to think about their own homes and to find things in the medieval homes that are similar to and things that are different from their homes. Provide students with a T chart for keeping track of their findings.

Demonstrating Understanding

Have students complete the organizer *What's the Difference?* on page 86 to record items from a medieval home and to compare them to similar items in their homes (e.g., a stone fireplace and a microwave; a medieval fireplace and a gas or electric fireplace). Ask students to think about why things were the way they were in Medieval Times and to record their deductions on the remaining section of the organizer. Deductions will probably be similar to the following:

- I think they used fire to cook with because there were no factories to make microwave ovens yet and no electricity to run them.
- Microwaves hadn't been discovered yet.

Comparing Data

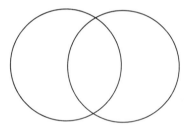

Venn diagram

Clarifying the Task

Comparing is a basic information skill that will have lifelong applications. Before students can compare though, they need two bodies of information, as well as common criteria or characteristics. In this task, the common characteristics are appearance, structure and functions/uses. Using this criteria, students explore the relationship of deciduous and coniferous trees and record how they are alike and how they are different on a Venn diagram.

Building Understanding

Introduce the topic by reading a picture book that demonstrates the importance of trees, such as the recently republished *A Tree Is Nice* (Janice May Urdy, 1956 and 2000). Following this, take your class outside and have students sketch their favorite tree in the schoolyard or neighborhood park. Start a list of kinds of trees. Talk about the parts of a tree and their functions and uses. Be sure to discuss the meaning of appearance, structure and functions/uses in contexts that will be familiar to the students (e.g., chair, apple, book, etc). Upon returning to class, chart the information the class has gathered about various trees.

To introduce the terms *deciduous* and *coniferous*, show a segment of a video. Using video is very effective because it offers an excellent way of reviewing prior learning (or introducing new concepts). Video is also an engaging resource that allows for a lot of information to be relayed in a short amount of time. After viewing, add to the earlier chart any new information that the students discovered in the video. At this point, ask the students to classify the trees on the chart as deciduous or coniferous. Confirm as necessary.

Schedule a time to work in the school library so students can further explore different kinds of trees. Ask students to select a tree they are interested in for their personal research. During their investigations, instruct students to record information about the appearance, structure and functions/uses of their tree on a triple T chart. Work with the teacher librarian to review and teach research skills as necessary.

When the research is complete, form groups that include a mix of students who investigated both coniferous and deciduous trees. Have them examine the information and look for similarities and differences. Provide students with highlighters or colored markers so they can physically identify similarities and differences. Show students how to transfer the information to the appropriate sections of a Venn diagram on paper or by using a computer application. If this is a new strategy for students, model the process with familiar objects as well.

Once the diagrams are complete, discuss similarities and differences discovered in order to confirm understanding of the classification terms *coniferous* and *deciduous*.

Demonstrating Understanding

Have the students complete written reflections on their learning about deciduous and coniferous trees and the process of making comparisons using a Venn diagram.

Identifying Relationships

Info Task
Students determine the major trading partners of their country and some products imported from those countries in order to identify relationships.

Clarifying the Task

It is important to help students link themselves and their immediate world with larger global issues. In this task, students start by gathering data about items found in their homes and then link this to statistical information. Using a web organizer will help them to discover relationships.

Building Understanding

Prepare students for a scavenger hunt survey, which they will conduct at home. Begin by giving students a simple T chart organizer. Ask them to take the organizer home and to select a variety of items (e.g., belt, teapot, watch, bike helmet, etc.) found in their home. Have them record on the T chart the names of about 20 items and the country they were manufactured in. Instruct students not to record items produced in their own country.

Item	Manufactured in . . .

Back in class, arrange students in groups to work with their lists to sort and classify the items and to record countries of origin. Instruct students to examine all the data from each member of their group to make some predictions about the major trading partners and the kinds of items they export to your country. Ask students how they can find out if their predictions are correct. Discuss and chart ideas from students. Arrange a time in the school library to work with the teacher librarian to discover the best sources of information for trading statistics.

Demonstrating Understanding

When students have gathered the data they need, have them work individually to create a web of major trading partners and the items that are imported. The organizer *Information Webbing* on page 87 can be used for this purpose.

Check It Out
When you study imports and exports, a web is an excellent way to visually represent the complexity of a country's import and export patterns. Using arrows and different kinds of information boxes, students will be able to see patterns and relationships.

Comparing Information Sources

Clarifying the Task

By gathering data from a variety of sources, students can gain a more balanced view of a topic. In this task students select and record key points from three different information sources in order to look for similarities and differences and conflicting information.

Building Understanding

Ask your students to work in groups to brainstorm as many places as they can think of where they can get information (e.g., books, Internet, encyclopedias, people, museums, telephone books, etc.). Give them adhesive notes or small strips of paper to record their ideas on so they are able to move them around. Ask the students to look for similarities and to cluster their information sources into different categories. Have them give each cluster or category a name.

Afterward, invite them to share and discuss their ideas. The following are some possible discussion questions:

> • Which information sources could you find here in your classroom, school or library?
> • Which information sources do you have at home?
> • What community resources are available to you?
> • Which sources do you like best for research? Why?
> • Why should we use more than one source for research?
> • How can we be sure that information is reliable?

Once they have finished the above activity, instruct your students to find three different types of resources for a project they are working on. Ask them to record key points using the organizer *Comparing Sources* on page 88. Explain that they should use the outside boxes to record key ideas they discover. Once students have exhausted all three resources, have them reread their key points and look for common information. If they find any points common to all three sources, ask the students to record them in the center box. Remind them that the wording does not have to be exactly the same. If they find conflicting information, have them rewrite it outside of the boxes. Ask students to think of ways to test out their conflicting information.

Demonstrating Understanding

Ask students to meet back in their groups and discuss what they have learned about research and different types of resources through this process. Have the students share and chart their findings. Individually, have each student create a chart on the computer of information sources they can use for research. Encourage them to put telephone numbers, Web addresses and other information on their chart where applicable. Have them print the charts and fasten them to their research folders for future reference.

Selecting Information

Info Task

Students locate and select information from a variety of resources in order to investigate the significance of an historical event, such as the building of the Canadian Pacific Railroad on the development of Western Canada.

Clarifying the Task

Locating and selecting key data and ideas is fundamental to successful information processing. In this task students learn how to search through large amounts of information, how to select relevant data and ideas, and how to sort the data to solve an information problem.

Building Understanding

Discuss the term *significance* with the class. To determine the significance of an event, students must first examine the impact the event has on the community. Use a local event, like the opening of a new supermarket, to demonstrate impact on the community. Make sure that students recognize that there is an impact on a number of individuals and groups with a range of effects.

Following this, ask the students to think about the individuals and groups that a particular historical event, such as the building of the CPR, would impact on. Chart their ideas.

When they have completed this, have them fold a paper into four columns and head each column with a person or group that they think might have been affected by the event they are examining. Schedule several sessions for your students to work in the school library to search for information on the event. You may need to have the teacher librarian review search strategies with your class. Remind students to keep their defined need in mind and to stay focused on the significance of the event (e.g., how the building of the CPR affected the development of Western Canada). Also, remind students to select a variety of resources on the topic (e.g., encyclopedias, reference materials and multimedia resources) so they see different perspectives.

Coach students to skim resources and scan for relevant passages, chapter headings, sub-topics, captions, etc., and then select a few to read more closely. Give students a quantity of adhesive notes so they can make reference notes about key points or questions they have about their discoveries. Instruct students to refer back to their adhesive notes, to read passages more closely and to select relevant data that is effective evidence for each heading on their organizer. As students record their data in point form, instruct them to keep it organized under the headings. Have students repeat this procedure with each resource. Encourage students to seek other sources if they are not satisfied with what they have found.

Afterward, group students so they can discuss and consult as they work with their information. Instruct groups to look for patterns and trends in their collective data. Have them select the three big ideas that they have discovered about the significance of the event, record supporting evidence and build a chart with their data using the organizer *Ranking Information* on page 89. Encourage students to dig for ripple effects as they identify those impacted.

Demonstrating Understanding

Have students individually demonstrate their understanding by writing a letter from the point of view of one of the individuals affected by the event they have examined to someone who is unfamiliar with the event. Giving students the opportunity to empathize helps them build real understanding of historical issues.

Check It Out

Make connections to literature through the powerfully illustrated fiction of Paul Yee.

CHAPTER THREE

Working with Information and Testing Ideas

In the tasks in this chapter, students scrutinize information in order to develop a clear understanding of what it means. Students also learn to look very closely at certain aspects of information to determine the connections. In their quest to fully understand, they need to bounce ideas with others and discuss different interpretations. Although often noisy, if well structured, activities such as these can help students clarify difficult concepts. A repertoire of group and collaborative skills will contribute to success.

As students work with information, prompts for thinking and questioning are effective springboards for new ideas. In discovering new ideas, students may discover aspects of a topic that require further investigation.

Students must experiment with information, look at it closely and think about it, in order to fully understand it. Deconstructing information empowers students to use it effectively.

The tasks that follow provide activities for students to:

- Explore and discover interesting aspects to focus on
- Create statements or questions to guide them to higher-level investigations
- Develop focused questions to extract precisely the information they need
- Clarify their ideas about the information by making inferences and predictions
- Investigate causes and their effects
- Make connections and reflect on the broad picture to discover impact
- Discuss, confer, challenge and reflect to clarify impressions
- Survey and interview to collect data
- Identify and investigate situations and issues
- Interpret data to extract information, make meaning and develop understanding

Developing a Focus

Clarifying the Task
This task leads students through a process of exploring the breadth and depth of a topic and narrowing it down to a personal inquiry.

Building Understanding
After students have experienced many exploratory activities on habitats they need opportunities to link this new topic to prior learning. Give your students activities in which they can work with each other to recall information and discuss ideas.

Teach students how to explore a topic through brainstorming lots of questions about it. To do this, select a habitat to model the process (e.g., coral reefs). Ask students what they would like to find out about the habitat. For example, what are they curious about? Using an LCD panel and commercial software, acetate on an overhead projector or simple chart paper, record student questions. As students are sharing questions, organize them and build on them by adding more questions, as well as information students recall.

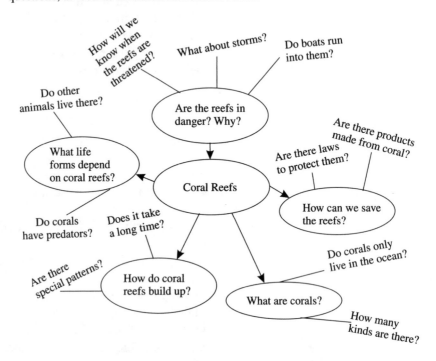

Next, provide your students with the *Topic Storming* organizer on page 90. Instruct students to select a habitat they are interested in and to begin topic storming. You will discover that it is much easier for students to narrow down a large topic and zero in on a manageable inquiry focus using this strategy. Ask students to highlight the phrases, words and questions that particularly interest them. Instruct them to carry on using the organizer to develop an inquiry question and sub-topics to focus their work. Finally, have them develop a list of keywords to help them with searches.

Demonstrating Understanding
Set up peer conferencing for your students so they can articulate their plans for research and try out their ideas on each other. Schedule consultations with them to check that students are on track and ready to proceed with the rest of their information gathering.

Check It Out
Have students analyze the effectiveness of their chosen keywords by the number of relevant hits in their electronic searches.

Formulating Questions

Info Task

Students formulate questions in order to focus their research so that they can develop an understanding of the significance of the St. Lawrence River and Great Lakes System.

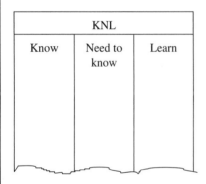

KNL		
Know	Need to know	Learn

Check It Out

For more strategies related to developing questioning skills, try using the organizers *Topic Storming* and *Defining Information Needs* on pages 90 and 91. For more information on focus words and developing questions, see a resource such as *Information Power Pack Junior Skillsbook* (Koechlin and Zwaan, 1997).

Clarifying the Task

The formulation of research questions is a prerequisite of successful information processing. Learning about different kinds of questions and their purposes can help increase skills in this area. In this task, students use some new strategies to help them formulate questions to facilitate their gathering and clarifying of information about the St. Lawrence River and the Great Lakes System.

Building Understanding

Engage the students in an exploration of the St. Lawrence River and the Great Lakes System using books, videos, pamphlets, posters and selected Internet sites. Provide students with a focus and purpose for each of the exploratory activities. Design a collaborative activity to help students make connections, sort ideas and narrow down the large topic to something more specific that they are curious about.

Ask students to work individually to record what they know already about their chosen topic, what they would like to find out, and where they can obtain more information, keywords and word strings that they can use for searches. Have students use an organizational strategy (e.g., KNL chart) to keep their ideas organized.

Review levels of questioning and practise developing questions at different levels. Provide students with lots of examples of questions at different levels. Four levels of questions to consider are:

- Questions which generate facts
- Questions which prompt analysis
- Questions which lead to original ideas
- Questions which prompt reflection

Encourage students to generate several questions at each level for the "need to know" section of their inquiry. As students gather data, they can check off sources they have explored and star or highlight questions from their list that they are becoming really interested in. These questions may become the focus for their inquiry.

Demonstrating Understanding

Before students are ready to launch into their data gathering, they need to refine their inquiry question/statement. Provide students with a rubric or checklist of desired criteria for effective inquiry questions, such as the *Questioning Rubric* provided on page 92. Discuss the criteria and ask students to create the question that will guide their research. Follow this with peer and teacher conferencing to prompt student reflection and assess their success.

Making Inferences

Info Task

Students analyze a news article to make inferences about the kinds of questions reporters use to gather information to write a news item.

Clarifying the Task

In this task students are asked to do some backward thinking. They take evidence from an article, make inferences about the reporter's information needs and intent, and generate a series of questions that a reporter would have had to ask in order to get the information required to compose the existing article.

Building Understanding

Tell students that they are going to assume the role of an apprentice reporter. Explain that they are in training to learn how to write news reports and that the first skill they will learn is preparing questions.

Gather short topical news items or magazine articles that will support a curriculum area. Make sure that the articles chosen are of interest to the students and at appropriate reading levels. Distribute the articles to the students. It is suggested that you group students in pairs or small groups to work. They will benefit from each other's experiences and perspectives.

Ask the students to read and discuss the articles and to underline or highlight key content — both facts and ideas/opinions. Using these key points, instruct students to create the questions that they think the reporter would have asked at the scene or interview to generate the information reported. Students will need to:

- Think backwards to what came before
- Try to empathize with the reporter (i.e., walk in his/her shoes)
- Read between the lines to determine the questions that resulted in reported ideas/opinions
- Make inferences about the aims and objectives of the reporter

If students need prior instruction in creating effective questions, see the Info Task *Formulating Questions* on page 35.

Demonstrating Understanding

Instruct groups to exchange their articles and corresponding questions. Ask each group to answer the "reporter's" questions from the original text. Encourage groups to add other questions if they feel the author asked more or different questions to generate the raw data needed to write the article. Have groups return articles and questions to the original teams.

As budding reporters, invite students to individually generate more questions that they would have liked answered if they had been the reporter at the scene (i.e., issues not addressed in the article). As students are working, consider:

- Do students understand what makes a question effective?
- Are students able to create effective questions?
- Can students make connections between the construction of a question and the reporter's intent?

Check It Out

As a warm-up activity, have students practise questioning with games such as "Jeopardy" and "Twenty Questions."

Making Predictions

Info Task
Students make inferences about a selected article or articles based on clues taken from the text. They then make predictions about the content of the article(s) based on the evidence they have.

Check It Out

This process can be used for newspaper articles, magazine articles, sections from textbooks and electronic sources. It is also an engaging way to introduce students to new novels. On the outside of an envelope record the title of the book, author, publisher and copyright date. In the envelope, provide cards containing keywords, a few character names, and important events, dates or phrases. Using this strategy you can introduce students to many new novels and it is a nice change from traditional book talks. It also gives students an opportunity to transfer the skills of making inferences and predictions.

Clarifying the Task

Much information today is very visual and organized to provide the consumer with a quick overview of the content (e.g., headings, symbols, hypertext links, sidebars, etc.). It is important, therefore, for students to learn and to practise inferring and predicting from textual clues. This task provides students with experiences to help develop these information skills.

Building Understanding

Organize the class into groups of four or five. Give each group an envelope of keywords and important phrases taken from the text of a short article. We suggest 10-15 words or phrases to give students the clues and evidence they will need to draw inferences and make predictions. Record the title of the article, the author's name, the publication name and the date on the outside of the envelope. You may wish to have groups working on the same article, or you may choose to distribute a variety of articles to ensure that students are exposed to alternative perspectives on an issue.

Ask the students to sort and cluster word/phrase cards to help them see relationships and make connections. The following question prompts provide scaffolding for this learning process:

> • What do you know already about the article from the information on the envelope?
> • How current is the information?
> • What can you determine about the writer's credibility?
> • What connections can you make with the word cards?
> • What ideas might be explored in this article?
> • Whose perspective seems to be represented?
> • Is there a bias evident? What and whose?
> • What is the intent or purpose of this piece?

Instruct the groups to work as teams to analyze the data they have about the article(s), to form inferences based on evidence, and to make predictions based on these inferences. Ask them to record their predictions on one side of a T chart and then to read the article(s) individually. Invite students to discuss the inferences they made in light of their reading and to correct or confirm their predictions on the remaining section of the T chart. You may need to review group work rules and routines before commencing.

Demonstrating Understanding

Debrief by asking each group to report on their discoveries and on the process. Watch to see if students have been able to make logical inferences and predictions from the clues given. Ask students to work individually to complete a learning log entry about their learning in this task.

Developing Generalizations

Info Task
Students investigate information technologies and make generalizations about their major functions.

Clarifying the Task

To help students wade through the glut of information that is available to them today, we need to give them practise with strategies that will help them make some quick generalizations. In this task, students learn to connect their own knowledge to new information. They learn how to break down a lot of information into categories and how to build personal understanding by putting it back together again in a visual generalization.

Building Understanding

Introduce the topic of information technology with an activity that will build common understanding of what it is. Have students clip pictures of information technologies from newspapers, magazines and flyers. Remind students to ask which materials are "clippable" so that they don't get into trouble with librarians and family members.

Book time with your teacher librarian so students can look for resources on information technologies. Remind students that people are resources too. For example, they could talk to people who design, sell or use information technologies.

Organize students into groups and have them sketch or record on adhesive notes the names of the information technologies they have discovered. In their groups, have students identify and discuss the uses of each technology. Remind students of their roles and responsibilities for group activities.

Give each group a large piece of chart paper. Ask them to sort the technologies by moving the adhesive notes around on the paper and clustering them according to their functions. Have students give each category a label (e.g., communication, research, entertainment, etc.). At this point your students will discover that many technologies have more than one function. Give students colored markers so they can link technologies to more then one function if appropriate. If students are having difficulty agreeing on categories and functions, a whole-class discussion might facilitate decision making.

Demonstrating Understanding

Have students pool their clippings and sketches to create a bulletin board web that represents the multiple functions of information technologies. Provide students with colored paper and yarn or string so they can visually represent their discoveries. Take a photograph of the web and enlarge and photocopy it so each student has a record for his or her notebook or portfolio.

Check It Out
Invite students to consider the advantages and disadvantages of different types of information technologies.

Working Collaboratively

Info Task

Students use appropriate strategies to organize their information and solve problems related to carrying out group projects.

Clarifying the Task

When students work as a team they can benefit from the skills, talents and perspectives of all the members. This task is designed to help students build effective skills for research that requires critical thinking and problem solving.

Building Understanding

Ask students for examples of teams in work situations, at home, and at play. Record them on a chart. Pose the question: What makes a team successful?

Ask the students to each select one example from the chart and jot down how they might know if that team is working successfully together (e.g., Band: they meet regularly to practise; everyone is on time; they all keep their instruments in good shape; they appear to enjoy playing together; people love to hear them play). In small groups, have the students share their successful group stories and look for common elements. Afterward, chart these common elements with the class. Cluster ideas and build consensus on the key elements of successful group work.

Provide students with the requirements for an information-related group project of your choice — format, completion dates for each stage of the process, student expectations and assessment criteria. Ensure that students understand the implications of the project requirements that they have been provided with. Organize students into groups for their projects.

Invite each group to discuss how they are going to implement the key elements of successful teamwork determined previously. Remind the students to identify the roles and responsibilities for each member. Explain that they will also need to establish strategies to solve group-related problems. Have them record their plan and make copies for each group member to refer to in their project folder.

Demonstrating Understanding

Conference with each group as often as possible. Have students complete individual and group assessments of their progress in working as a team periodically throughout the process. The organizer *Assessing Group Work Skills* on page 93 can help with this.

Check It Out

"When graphic organizers, thinking skills and cooperative learning are combined, they create a powerful synergy which is whole-brain compatible." For more on this, see *Designing Brain Compatible Learning* (Terrance and Gregory, 1998).

Clarifying Understanding

Clarifying the Task

In this task students clarify their understanding about the distinguishing features of a medieval society. It is a good idea to present a broad spectrum of medieval cultures when preparing for this task. Because of the reading level and complexity of most information texts on this topic, we recommend "learning buddies" to assist students.

Building Understanding

Ask students to think about features that are important in their own community (e.g., education, clothing, design and technology, transportation, commerce and trade, housing, etc.). Discuss examples of each feature. Using this information, review and chart the basic features of any society.

Prepare students to work in groups to investigate a basic feature of medieval society. Borrow older students from another class to work with the groups as "learning buddies." The ratio of buddies to each group will depend on the specific needs of students in your class. Conduct a separate session with the learning buddies to explain the expectations of their role (e.g., helping students to use indexes, conduct on-line searches, select relevant data, etc.). As the students collect and reflect on their discoveries, provide them with copies of the organizer *Clarifying Understanding* on page 94 to record on.

When each group has investigated its feature of medieval society, prepare a jigsaw grouping to share the learning. Appoint a "learning buddy" to each group to facilitate the sharing and discussion. Learning buddies may need an overview of the jigsaw strategy.

Demonstrating Understanding

Ask each group to create a web of its understanding of the features of medieval society. If this is the first time students have created webs, model the process with them using their own community.

Check It Out

For information on using the jigsaw strategy, log on to Jigsaw Classroom at www.jigsaw.org/.

Clarifying Meaning

Clarifying the Task

In this task students work collaboratively in groups to clarify the meaning of knowledge and concepts by building on the ideas of others. Students learn how to listen to and respond constructively to alternative ideas and viewpoints.

Building Understanding

Group students in small clusters of three or four. Explain to the students that in this activity they are going to practise the skill of paraphrasing to help clarify meaning.

To begin, review group work skills such as:

- Listening without interrupting
- Being aware of other people's feelings
- Giving physical reinforcement (e.g., head nods, smiles)
- Responding to new ideas
- Encouraging others
- Accepting responsibility for tasks

Assign each group a media piece to read, view or listen to, and provide students with some think time. Once the students are familiar with the text, ask the first student in the group to summarize the text and add a personal statement in response to the text. Next, ask the second student to paraphrase and respond to or extend the first student's response. Finally, ask the third student to paraphrase student two's response, extend the thinking again, and so forth.

Provide reflection prompts to assist students when paraphrasing. For example:

- I think you are saying ...
- So, you are saying ...
- Am I understanding you to say ... ?
- You are thinking that ...
- I heard you say that ...
- You're suggesting that ...
- To summarize, I think you said ...

Demonstrating Understanding

Ask the students to complete a learning log entry that will require them to reflect critically on this process of working in a group to help clarify the meaning of new information. Offer some learning log prompts such as:

- It was encouraging when ...
- I found it difficult to ...
- It helped me when ...
- I kept forgetting to ...
- I feel this helped me to ...
- Now I understand ...
- Next time I would ...

Check It Out

For more about how to make group work effective for your class, consult a resource such as *Information Power Pack Junior Skillsbook* (Koechlin and Zwaan, 1997). For ideas on how to use the collaborative process to integrate computers, see *Computer Activities for the Cooperative Classroom* (Schwartz and Willing, 2001).

Clarifying Thinking

Clarifying the Task

By asking questions and discussing different aspects of information with their classmates, students are able to clarify their thinking and learn to contribute to and work constructively in groups. This, in turn, can lead to better preparation for quizzes and tests. Before beginning this task, consider whether the students would benefit from a review of group work skills and strategies.

Building Understanding

Present a slogan such as "work smarter — not harder." Ask students to brainstorm strategies for improving the quality of their study time (e.g., management of time, the creation of a place to study, exercise, rest, attention to nutrition, reading and rereading, etc.). As well, invite students to rethink the way they traditionally study and to try out something new.

During class time, teach students how to review material and study using a variety of skills and strategies, such as those listed here:

- Point-form notes
- Outlining
- Webbing
- Highlighting
- Adhesive notes or index cards
- Sketches and diagrams
- Paraphrasing
- Questioning
- Mnemonics (memory improvement techniques such as rhymes, silly sentences or acronyms)
- SQ4R (survey, question, read, recite, write, review)
- E-mail conferencing

Set up "study groups" so that the students get a chance to try out some new techniques.

Demonstrating Understanding

After trying out some new study techniques and then writing some quizzes and tests, ask students to review their success and to set goals for improvement. Consider:

- Would a T chart help them compare current habits and suggested new habits?
- Could students use a checklist of study suggestions to track the strategies they use?
- Were there some strategies that students thought worked better for them than others?

Check It Out

For ideas to help students set goals, manage time, organize work areas, prepare for exams and generally take responsibility for their own learning, consult a resource such as *Information Power Pack Intermediate Skillsbook* (Koechlin and Zwaan, 1997).

Discussing Ideas

Clarifying the Task

Testing ideas by consulting, discussing, listening, responding and reflecting will help students develop understanding. This task provides a structure for learning how to interact with others to process information.

Building Understanding

The following strategy can be used when responding to any curriculum issue. Introduce the chosen issue using a video, a presenter, a field trip or printed text. Afterward, provide students with time to think about what they have discovered during this experience, what they don't understand, and what they still need to know or want to know.

Introduce the consultation process as a strategy for testing ideas and problem solving. Discuss the role of a consultant in the business world. Ask students to think about what attributes and specialized skills a consultant needs to possess. Discuss how a businessperson would prepare to use the services of a consultant. Instruct students to prepare for discussion by recording their initial responses to the curriculum issue on the *Consultation Process* organizer on page 95.

Next, organize students for the "Expert Line Strategy." For this strategy, you will need to set up two rows of chairs facing one another. Students in Row A are the experts: they will start by answering questions. Students in Row B are seeking help. Time each consultation period. Signal the stop time. At this point, have students in Row B stand up and move a chair to the right. Consultation then begins again. Continue for four or five sessions and then reverse roles so that Row B students become the experts and Row A students are seeking help.

This activity can be varied by having the students stand rather than use chairs or by forming a double circle. Although this is a noisy activity, the results are well worth it.

Demonstrating Understanding

Have students return to their *Consultation Process* organizer and respond to new understandings and record new questions arising as a result of their interactions with others. Ask students also to consider viewpoints that confirmed or conflicted with theirs.

Ensure that there is adequate time to debrief with students. Consider:

• What is their understanding of the issue now?
• What could be done about it?

Clarifying Ideas

Clarifying the Task

In this task, students apply organizational and communication skills when conferencing with a partner in order to clarify understanding of a topic or issue and to solve problems. The strategy presented below is designed to encourage efficient organization before a conference begins, effective communication during a conference, and reflection on the conferencing process.

Building Understanding

Brainstorm occasions when it is helpful to work with a partner (e.g., working on an experiment, a computer task or a math problem). Discuss why working with a partner is often beneficial. Explain that conferencing with a partner is a particularly useful technique for helping students to work with ideas and solve problems.

Introduce these four easy steps for conferencing successfully with a partner:

- *Prepare* for the conference. Plan and practise what you want to share/ discuss/test out. Organize your materials, research notes, drafts, writing, drawings, etc.
- *Share* your work. Present your hypothesis, show your slideshow, etc. Ask for input from your partner.
- *Practise* your communication skills. Focus on critical reading, active listening, active viewing, questioning, responding and encouraging.
- *Reflect* on the conference. Record new ideas, plans to adjust your research or presentation, and goals for yourself.

Have students practise the four steps of conferencing using a selection from a textbook or periodical related to a current curriculum topic. Students can conference with a learning buddy, a teacher, a teacher librarian, a parent, a school volunteer, etc. Some students may require prompts to help them with the reflection step. You may wish to have a large poster-sized sample of the four steps of conferencing made to display in the room or a bookmark-style version of the steps prepared for students to carry with them.

Demonstrating Understanding

Ask students to write a thank-you letter to their conference partner, expressing what they discovered from the experience. Consider:

- Were the students able to identify discoveries that related to the advantages of conferencing with a partner?
- Did they identify negatives?
- Did they offer suggestions for improving their next experience?

Check It Out
For ideas on transferring these skills to student-led conferencing with parents, see *Together Is Better* (Davies, Cameron, Politano and Gregory, 1992).

Designing Surveys

Info Task

Students design a survey to collect information from their families and friends about how water is used in their homes.

Clarifying the Task

Designing and conducting a survey is a powerful way for students to acquire primary information on a topic. Sometimes it is the only method of acquiring current data. The process needs to be carefully structured to ensure student success.

Building Understanding

Discuss with the class what kind of information they need to gather to find out how water is used in people's homes. In small groups have students brainstorm and record possible survey questions on individual cue cards. Share the questions and post so everyone can see the cards.

Ask students to look for similar questions and to move the cards to cluster these questions. With the class, decide on one question in each cluster that will become a survey question. Students may need to rework questions, combining parts of several to create one comprehensive question. As a class, decide how many questions there will be and the order of questioning. Create an organizer with the questions on it, as well as space for students to record answers.

Instruct students to rehearse conducting the survey taking turns as questioner and interviewee. Provide specific instructions with regard to the purpose, times and people to be surveyed. Remind students of etiquette and safety rules.

Ask students to make predictions about the information they think they will get in response to their survey questions. Upon completing the surveys, have students work in small groups to share their findings, analyze the results and record the results visually (e.g., graphs, charts, etc.).

Demonstrating Understanding

In small groups, have students compare their results with their earlier predictions. Encourage students to discuss reasons for the survey results, variations they discovered, confirmations they made and conflicting data. Have each student complete a learning log entry which prompts them to think about the survey process itself and the actions they can take to address concerns about water use in homes.

As you assess this task, consider whether students are able to:

- Link their predictions to the data they gathered
- Articulate how the survey process works, what problems they encountered and what successes they had
- Explain why they got the results that they did
- Account for some variations in the data
- Use the information gained from the survey and apply it to a need for conservation measures or use it to promote models of conservation
- Develop realistic action plans to address the concerns raised by the survey

Check It Out

Collect samples of a variety of surveys for students to analyze.

Determining Cause

Info Task

Students investigate the reactions of the members of their class and other classes to a variety of popular television programs in order to discover the cause(s) of these responses.

Clarifying the Task

Students need to go through the process of collecting and analyzing information before they are able to determine cause. In this task, students first survey their peers to collect needed primary data. They then organize and examine their results in order to explain their own and their peers' reactions to specific television programs.

Building Understanding

Show video segments from a variety of genres (e.g., mystery, romance, adventure and musical). After each segment ask students to complete two reflections you have selected from the organizer *Reacting to Media* on page 96. Form student groups to analyze the responses to each media segment. Have the students sort and cluster the reflections and suggest reasons/causes for the reactions.

Next, ask students to brainstorm a list of television programs they like to watch. Ask them to select six or seven to focus on for this investigation. Remind students to select programs that are representative of the wide variety of programs watched by class members.

Working in small groups of three or four, have students create survey prompts to collect the data needed for the investigation. Ask each group to create two prompts for one of the programs. Prompts should be similar to those following:

Program A

I was upset when _____ because it reminded me of _____.
_____was exciting. It was like _____.

Program B

I'm glad I'm not _____. I wouldn't want to _____.
I enjoyed _____, however _____.

After combining the prompts to create a common survey, do a review of the survey prompts to identify overlap, make revisions and determine what is still required to round out the survey. As students review their survey, ask them to consider:

- Do your prompts call for a feeling and an association or reaction?
- Have you included prompts that will identify a range of emotions and opinions?
- Have you crafted prompts that will help you discover the reasons for the different reactions of your class members?

Ask students to fill out the survey themselves and to ask a set number of friends in other classes to also complete it.

Demonstrating Understanding

Reassemble student groups to examine and summarize the data collected for a selected television program. Encourage each group to identify the range of reactions and to discuss the reasons for the different reactions. Remind the groups to work with the data they have collected to draw conclusions and determine the cause(s) of the reactions. Have each group create a visual that represents the range of reactions to the program and possible causes for those reactions (e.g., web or graph). Share visuals from each group and encourage discussion.

Check It Out

Try using the reflection prompts from *Reacting to Media* on page 96 for literature circle discussions and book reports. These will really indicate how well a student has connected with a story.

Investigating Effect

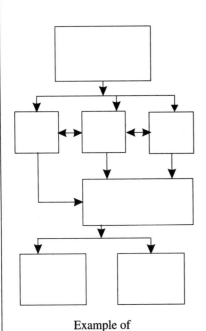

Example of
Flow Chart

Clarifying the Task

Music affects various aspects of society. In this task students gather primary data and build on that data by researching a particular aspect of the music industry. Collaboratively, the class discovers the ripple effect that the music community has on society.

Building Understanding

Give the students a homework assignment in the form of a scavenger hunt to locate evidence of music in their community. Direct students to look for a wide variety of music events and related activities. As a class, share what they have discovered.

Using this information, have students work in small groups to create music webs. Ensure that all aspects of music in the community are represented in the webs. Encourage students to look for links and ripple effects. They should make links to industry, entertainment, education, social life, marketing, media and employment. Suggest that they add more data as they build their web and make new connections.

As a class, determine several categories (e.g., recording, marketing, performances) for further investigation. Afterward, ask students to return to their small groups and to investigate one category. Explain that each group will need to develop a question or statement of inquiry to focus its investigation (e.g., How does the recording industry affect my community?). Have each student use the organizer *Investigating Effect* on page 97 as a framework for analyzing the effect on the community.

Demonstrating Understanding

In their groups, direct students to produce a flow chart to help them visualize the extent of the effect their chosen aspect of music has on their community. Post flow charts and share findings. Have the students compare the flow charts and look for links or relationships among them.

Determining Effect

Info Task

Students develop an appropriate question to guide their research on how human activity affects the environment.

Clarifying the Task

The success of this information task depends on the quality of the questions that students develop. Students use a rubric to help them develop higher-level questions. After constructing a question to guide the rest of their research, students then use a graphic organizer to help them analyze the effect of a recreational activity on the environment from several viewpoints.

Building Understanding

Brainstorm with the students recreational activities that are enjoyed by members of their community. Remind students to include activities that are both indoor and outdoor, team-oriented and individual, organized and informal, and requiring specialized equipment or little or no equipment. Encourage students to work in groups to share, sort and categorize their information in order to enhance their repertoire. Using this information as a resource, ask each student to select one recreational activity to investigate.

Ask students individually to develop a question to guide their own quest for information on how their recreational activity affects the environment. Provide students with the *Questioning Rubric* on page 92 and draw attention to evaluation criteria and indicators for success. Discuss the use of specific words to help focus a question and words to help direct the making of relationships. Have students self-evaluate their question using the rubric. Work with students individually to further develop their question until they are ready to proceed with their investigation. See the Info Task *Formulating Questions* on page 35 for more ideas about helping students develop research questions.

Afterward, direct students to individually locate, select and retrieve information about the recreational activity that they have chosen, using their question to guide them. Arrange with the teacher librarian for students to have time in the library to collect the information they need. Encourage students to phone, fax, consult, etc.

As your students are working, consider whether they have:

- Selected effective keywords
- Used a variety of sources
- Collected all the necessary types of information (e.g., Does the activity require a special setting such as ice, water, large open field or track?)
- Identified what happens to the surrounding area as a result of this activity?
- Considered things like changes made to traffic, garbage, potential for fire, personal injury, accidents, pollution, etc?
- Made connections to the economy of the area and the related social effects?

Provide students with the organizer *Determining Effect* on page 98 to record and sort their information and to reflect on their findings.

Demonstrating Understanding

Direct students to use their findings in a mock presentation to a local recreation board to lobby for or against the recreational activity. Provide students with tips for presenting an argument.

Check It Out

After students have had experiences self-evaluating with rubrics, try teaching them to develop criteria. See a book such as *Setting and Using Criteria* (Gregory, Cameron and Davies, 1997) for more information on this.

Predicting Effect

Info Task
Students explore the changes that urban development brings to a community. They then predict the effects these changes may have on the local environment.

Clarifying the Task

In this task students practise applying "The pinball effect" in order to explore ways in which urban development can affect the natural world. Students will need to have a working knowledge of urban development issues as background for this information task.

Building Understanding

Select a video segment or a piece of text that provides a good overview of the changes urban development brings to a community. Instruct your students to view the video segment or read the piece of selected text to a predetermined point. Ask them to individually record several changes they discovered in the video or information piece on adhesive notes or index cards. Set up small groups of students to share their data and to begin to discuss the possible implications each of these changes may have on the environment.

Have the students work individually to begin to analyze the data on a chart where they record each change, possible implications and predictions of the future effects of the changes.

Predictions About Urban Development		
Changes	Possible Implications	Predicted Effects

Afterward, ask the students to view/read the rest of the text. Direct them to confirm or disprove their personal predictions using the selected text. Students may need to seek out other sources to further test their predictions. Check to make sure your students are stretching their thinking to identify both positive and negative implications.

Demonstrating Understanding

Return students to their groups so they can share their anticipated implications, effects and any verifications they were able to make. Instruct the groups to prepare a "pinball effect" web that will illustrate their predicted effects, the ripple effects and the connections they have discovered.

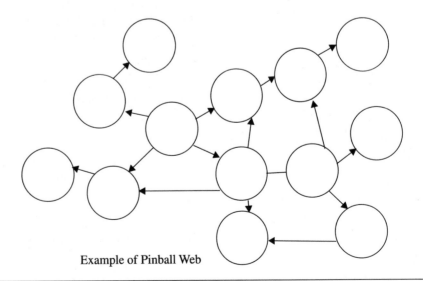

Example of Pinball Web

Check It Out
To extend the learning potential of this task and to make the experience more authentic for your students, ask each group to prepare a short dramatization. Instruct them to assume the roles of citizens expressing their concerns about the effects of urban development in their community. Remind students to explore a variety of perspectives on the issue in their drama.

Discovering Impact

Info Task

Students discover how major inventions and discoveries of the twentieth century have impacted on society.

Clarifying the Task

The first step in discovering the impact — or powerful effect — of an invention is to gather data about it. The next step is to determine who and what was affected and how each was affected by the invention. This task models a process of gathering and organizing the background information and provides an organizer for scaffolding student discovery of impact.

Building Understanding

Introduce the topic with a story such as *The Real McCoy: The Life of an African-American Inventor* by Wendy Towle (1995) to spark interest and thinking. Discuss the immediate effects this invention had on the railway industry. Revisit sections of the text as necessary to locate specific information about the effects of this invention.

Use an enlarged version of the organizer *Discovering Impact* on page 99 to record who and what was affected. If necessary, read aloud specific sections of the text to determine how each was affected. Discuss the implications of these effects. Record the students' ideas in the appropriate remaining columns.

Afterward, ask the students to describe their impression of the impact this invention had on society. Discuss the links between the effects on people and things and the ultimate impact on a larger scale. Once the students have experienced this modeling of the process they should be ready to try it on their own.

Ask students to tell about other inventors and discoveries they are aware of. Collectively chart these inventors, inventions and/or discoveries. Show a video or a video clip on the topic and instruct students to jot down anything that is not already on the chart. Debrief and add new discoveries and inventions to the chart.

Assign students to groups and book time in the school library where they can work with you and the teacher librarian to further explore this topic. Prepare or have the students create a chart so they can record their discoveries and begin the process of discovering the impact of these events on society. For example:

Inventor	Invention/ Discovery	Importance	Source

After a defined time period, instruct groups to select one inventor from their chart that they are really curious about. Have students investigate resources to dig a little deeper into the effects and larger impact of this invention/discovery on society. Encourage students to use the organizer *Discovering Impact* on page 99 to guide the processing of their information. As a class, share the results.

Check It Out

Students need to keep track of their sources so they can refer back to them if they need more information. Teach students how to record sources they have used on organizers or on index cards. Remind students to keep all this information in a research folder so they won't lose it.

Demonstrating Understanding

Have students individually complete these reflections:

- I didn't know that _____ perhaps _____
- The most interesting invention/discovery for me is _____ because _____
- I would like to be_____ because _____
- If _____ hadn't been invented/discovered then _____
- I wonder if_____

Considering Alternatives

Clarifying the Task

Students need to practise their information processing skills by applying them to real world issues. This task uses a current issue of global interest — water resource use — and leads students through a problem-solving process. It also provides them with a forum for demonstrating their understanding in an authentic way.

Building Understanding

Brainstorm uses of water resources. You may need to provide students with some exploratory experiences to broaden their background knowledge of the topic. Work with the students to sort and categorize their ideas.

Direct the students to select an area of interest regarding water use (e.g., bottled water) and then to conduct an investigation and record relevant information. Ensure that students explore the topic using a wide variety of current resources. Determining the validity of resources used will be critical to this task. Book time with your teacher librarian to review how to validate sources and to assist with locating the best resources for this topic.

Ask the students to analyze the viability of the practice they investigated and to consider alternatives using the organizer *Problems/Issues* on page 100. Check that the alternatives selected by students represent a range of perspectives and a range of kinds of uses such as domestic, industrial, commercial, recreational and natural. After discussing the organizer and its evaluation with the students, have them use it to prepare for their demonstration of understanding.

Demonstrating Understanding

Ask each student to assume the role of spokesperson for a group concerned about water resources and to prepare a brief press release to be presented at a mock news conference about alternative water uses. Invite another class to participate in the mock news conference.

Divide each class into groups of 5 or 6. Arrange time for the spokespeople to present their press releases to the groups of students attending the news conference as press agents. Explain that the press agents are allowed to question the presenters. Make sure that the press agents are also aware of the issues surrounding managing water resources effectively to ensure sustainability.

Observe the students to see if they are able to present and defend their alternatives for water use. Press agents may be able to assist in the assessment of press statements if they are provided with a rubric or checklist.

Check It Out

For more ideas on processing information about current issues, look at *Analyzing Issues* (Donald Galbraith, 1997).

Identifying and Investigating Trends

Info Task

Students conduct a survey to identify and investigate how current societal trends are affecting the growth and decline of certain jobs.

Clarifying the Task

Societal trends affect not only the types of jobs we do, but also the ways in which we work and try to balance work with family needs. Through the examination of existing data and data collected in a survey of adult family members, students can learn a lot about how societal trends are affecting employment patterns.

Building Understanding

Provide the students with information about trends that are resulting in changes in the job market (e.g., daycare, working from home). Discuss some of these trends.

Work with students to prepare questions for a survey that explores work both in the present and in previous generations. For example:

- What kind of work do/did you do?
- Who worked outside/inside the home in the past?
- Who works outside/inside the home today?
- Did you attend daycare when you were young?
- Do children in your own family attend daycare?
- Do/did older family members live at home?

Ask students to conduct the survey with adult members and to record their findings.

Back in class, have students input their findings into a simple database, create graphs and analyze their results. Encourage students to compare their data with the information on societal trends that you presented earlier to help identify relationships and patterns. Remind them to explore trends from a variety of perspectives (e.g., workers', shareholders', owners', customers', environmentalists', politicians', etc.).

Demonstrating Understanding

Ask students to complete a journal entry reflecting on their discoveries, the learning process, and how they can use this information to help shape their own career paths. As students organize and analyze their data, and complete their journal entries, consider:

- Do students have an organized way of collecting their data?
- Did they discover what I expected?/ what they expected?/ what the experts suggest?
- Are students addressing the full spectrum of possible effects (e.g., effects on wages, profits, number of jobs available, shifts worked, new demands for certain types of skilled workers, services and products, etc.)?

Check It Out

Students may wish to examine writings by futurists such as Frank Feather, David Foot, Alvin Tofler and Nuella Beck to see which trends may affect work in the future.

Interpreting Graphs and Charts

Info Task
Students create charts and graphs to display data about buying habits for interpretation.

Clarifying the Task
In this task students need to input a set of data into a familiar spreadsheet program, then create and evaluate a variety of charts and graphs to determine which best meets their needs. Once they have selected the most effective one, they will need to study it to interpret the information.

Building Understanding
Discuss with students the function of charts/graphs. Ask students to relate their experiences with graphs and charts in other subject areas, as well as personal applications.

Explain to students that for this task they will be using previously collected data on the buying habits of 500 area students regarding three different products, collected for the owner of a new variety store. Tell the students that their job will be to represent the data visually to help the storeowner make the best decisions regarding the amount of stock to order and to keep on hand.

Provide students with copies of both the *Raw Data for Interpretation* and the organizer *Interpreting and Evaluating Graphs and Charts* on page 101. To begin, have the students input the data for frozen treats into a database. Instruct the students to experiment by creating a variety of charts and graphs from the database. Have them print the one that most effectively illustrates information about the students' buying habits.

Raw Data for Interpretation												
	Jan	Feb	Mar	Apr	May	June	July	Aug	Sept	Oct	Nov	Dec
frozen treats	10	12	25	111	300	460	465	455	390	50	30	5
chewing gum	315	325	315	300	300	325	400	400	300	300	300	100
chocolate	225	350	225	220	95	75	70	70	95	195	225	150

Check It Out
If students have had limited experience creating or interpreting graphs and charts, collect a variety of samples from books, pamphlets, magazines, newspapers and the Internet. Have students sort and categorize the graphs and charts. Discuss their functions and effectiveness. Create a bulletin board display that highlights the advantages and disadvantages of different types of visual information. You could add pictures, maps and diagrams as well.

Explain that they are to record an evaluation of three graphs/charts and determine which is most effective. Reconvene as a group to discuss the advantages, disadvantages and interesting features of the graphs/charts they evaluated. Have students identify those selected as most effective and tally the results. Ask students to summarize the reasons for their choices. Consider whether they were able to justify their selections.

Have the students reconsider their selections taking into account the comments of other students. Allow the students time to individually study the graph/chart they selected and use the prompts on the organizer to help them determine what information they can glean from it to assist the store staff. Have them meet again as a group to share and summarize what they discovered and what they think it means for the store. Listen to their summaries, confirm their interpretations and provide guidance where necessary.

Demonstrating Understanding
Have students input the data for the other two products. Using data for all three product groups, have the students individually follow the same process to select the most useful graph/chart, interpret the information and summarize what is important to the store owner.

Constructing Organizers

Info Task
Students create a visual tool to organize data for analyzing.

Clarifying the Task

When students begin working with information they use teacher-prepared organizers to sort and record data in preparation for further analysis. As they begin to work with more complicated content, assignments often require personal investigation or reaction. At this point each student may require a slightly different organizer to support specific individual goals. In this task, after focused observation of many examples, students use a software program to construct an organizer that will facilitate analysis for an issues-related assignment.

Building Understanding

Review and list the uses of graphic organizers. Be sure to include categories such as sorting, classifying, mapping, comparing, breaking down, identifying connections and prompting reactions. Guide a group discussion to elicit connections between graphic organizers as tools of analysis and the processing of information. Have students relate experiences with organizers for a variety of subject areas and purposes.

Divide the class into groups of four or five and provide each group with a set of sample organizers, which represents a wide range of uses. See the appendix in *Info Tasks,* resources listed in Check It Outs and samples collected from colleagues to ensure that the set contains a wide variety of organizers.

Direct students to study the samples, discuss the purpose of each, and consider how they achieve their purpose. Provide them with some prompts similar to:

- What makes this organizer specific to the task?
- How does it help organize information for this task?
- How does this organizer help the user?
- What could be done to make it better?

Reconvene to share and record findings on a master chart for several high-level organizers.

Demonstrating Understanding

Explain to the students that they are expected to create an organizer for their own use in an upcoming assignment. Distribute and discuss the rubric *Creation and Use of Graphic Organizers* on page 102.

Guide the students to draw on their experiences with organizers and make connections to the statement of purpose or inquiry question for a current information assignment as they create their own organizer using the *Graphic Organizer Worksheet* on page 103 as a guide. Make arrangements for students to have access to computers and familiar software. Ask students to create a graphic organizer specific to their need and have them self evaluate the finished product using the *Creation and Use of Graphic Organizers* rubric.

Check It Out

To learn more about graphic organizers, see *Visual Tools for Constructing Knowledge* by David Hyerle and log on to *The Graphic Organizer* at www.graphic.org/ to connect to a wealth of resources.

CHAPTER FOUR

Analyzing and Synthesizing Findings and Drawing Conclusions

In these tasks students work with more complex analysis. By exploring aspects such as intent, bias, point of view and opinion, they begin to look for more subtle influences to the meaning and value of information. For example, they may discover how the presence of bias can discredit a piece of information, but can also serve as a powerful support for an argument. Students go beyond simple comparison to identify specific features so they can begin to make judgments and predictions, and draw conclusions.

By applying a variety of analytical strategies to a body of information students acquire the depth of understanding they need for synthesis. When people synthesize they use what they learned/discovered during analysis to create something new. Synthesis may include writing, inventing, creating, composing, planning, imagining, and much more. In using information to define their own ideas and understand their own reactions to information, students can begin to develop personal knowledge.

The tasks that follow help prepare students for analysis and synthesis by allowing them to:

- Make comparisons based on specific criteria
- Identify multiple relationships to interpret information
- Make observations and determine relationships to discover effect and importance
- Categorize information and organize it visually to build understanding
- Investigate reactions to information in order to interpret personal responses
- Examine illustrations to determine informational content
- Examine facts in controversial issues and identify interests of stake-holders to interpret spin
- Study the construction of ideas and the creator's intent to discover influence
- Consider fact and perspective to define personal views and opinions
- Study impact to make judgments
- Apply results of analysis to make decisions
- Identify and examine facts and perspectives to build personal knowledge
- Identify relationships between collected data and personal knowledge to make decisions

Examining Relationships

Info Task

Students record environmental sounds and collaboratively identify the purpose(s) of the sounds in order to discover how they relate to daily life.

Clarifying the Task

In this task, students identify various uses of sound encountered in daily life. After collecting sounds and details about the purpose(s) of the sounds, they are able to begin to examine the relationships these sounds have to each other and to the environment.

Building Understanding

Instruct groups of students to gather sounds on a tape recorder and note the sources of the sounds and their function(s) or purpose(s) on a T chart. Have the groups share the sounds they identified and create a collaborative list of sounds, eliminating all repetition.

Provide students with copies of the list to cut and manipulate so they can sort the sounds and arrange them on a sheet of chart paper. First, have them organize the sounds by their source. Ask students to label each cluster (e.g., music, traffic, learning, wildlife). Then, have the students gather the sounds, turn over the chart paper, and classify them again by purpose or use. Again, instruct the students to label the clusters (e.g., safety, pleasure, information, etc.).

Demonstrating Understanding

Have the students conference in their work groups and share their thoughts on what they learned about the sounds around them. Ask groups to again sort their "sounds" and identify the number of occurrences of:

- Sounds for enjoyment
- Sounds for safety
- Sounds from machines, equipment, traffic, etc.
- Sounds from nature

Monitor the discussion to discover whether the students express both the positive and negative aspects of sound, such as assisting blind pedestrians and noise pollution.

Afterward, ask students to individually interpret their information using a bar graph and then to complete the following reflections:

- I studied the sounds around me and I discovered that _____
  _____
- I feel that _____
  _____

Check It Out

Suggest that the groups select a category that they feel is important to them and create a soundscape (a collection of sounds that creates an atmosphere or enhances a scene) with their recorded sounds. Encourage them to share their soundscape with the class, along with their impressions of its importance. Groups could also write a story to accompany the soundscape and share it by creating a multimedia slide show.

Making Connections

Clarifying the Task

In this task, students explore why soil is important to humans and other living things. For students to make these connections they need to first discover information about kinds of soil and information about the uses of soil. Later, they use the strategy of webbing to relate their collective findings and discover the importance of soil.

Building Understanding

Introduce the topic of soil with a related video or picture book. Discuss and chart the uses of soil that were revealed using the resource. Next, take students on a soil search in the schoolyard/neighborhood to discover ways soil is used. Provide students with clipboards and recording sheets so they can keep track of their findings.

Back in the class, ask students to work in small groups to recall the evidence of uses of soil that they observed. Instruct students to begin analyzing their observations by building a web where they look at connections between soil uses and the needs of humans and other living things.

Model some examples of connections so students learn how to look at information from many angles. For example: soil is used for flower gardens which:

- Help make the neighborhood beautiful
- Provide flowers that are sold to earn money for gardeners
- Produce flowers that provide nectar for hummingbirds and insects
- Offer nectar to bees, which in turn make honey that can be sold

Encourage the students to create detailed webs that look at a variety of uses of soil and the importance of each of these. Afterward, provide student groups with a forum for sharing their analyses (e.g., reporting, posting, gallery walk, etc.).

Demonstrating Understanding

Have individual students complete the learning log organizer *Keeping Track of My Learning* on page 104 to reflect upon their learning in this task.

Check It Out

Try having students create a poem "The important thing about soil …" patterned after Margaret Wise Brown's *The Important Book* (1949 and 1999).

Evaluating Effects

Info Task

Students investigate sources of energy to evaluate the effects of their uses on natural and human-made environments.

Clarifying the Task

In this task students begin by researching possible energy sources, both renewable and non-renewable. They then seek to find out how these energy sources are used and to investigate the possible effects of each of these sources on the environment. Students share their learning by creating a computer slideshow to teach others the importance of conserving energy and investigating alternative energy sources.

Building Understanding

To conduct this inquiry, students will need access to a broad range of current resources. Develop with the teacher librarian a process for students to explore the broad topic of "sources of energy."

Once sources of energy have been discovered and sorted into renewable and non-renewable sources, assign students to groups to begin research on an energy source they want to investigate. Provide students with a contract for completion dates and conferencing at each stage of the research process. Ensure that all students are clear about the expectations and evaluation criteria for the research process and the final presentation. See the *Information Literacy Rubric* on page 10.

At the point where students have collected and examined their raw data, provide them with the organizer *Investigating Effect* on page 97. This tool can help them develop an understanding of the effect their energy source has on the environment and why that effect is important. This organizer can also provide the students with the basic framework for constructing the flow and connectivity of their slideshow. When the slideshows are complete, arrange for students to share their learning with other classes or mount their work on the school Web site and invite responses.

Demonstrating Understanding

Have students write letters to appropriate organizations expressing their concerns regarding the discoveries they made during their investigation. Provide students with the *Processing Rubric* on page 105 so they can self-assess their processing of information and set goals for personal improvement.

Check It Out

For more ideas on integrating technology into the curriculum see *Hyperlearning: Where Projects, Inquiry and Technology Meet* (Wilhelm, Friedemann and Erickson, 1998).

Determining Impact

Info Task
Students differentiate between the food production methods of developing and developed countries in order to identify the impact of those methods on food safety.

Clarifying the Task

In this task, in order to determine the impact of production methods on food safety, students have to:

- Collect data related to certain criteria for two countries
- Find similarities and differences
- Discover the importance and effects of the data for both countries
- Make both positive and negative connections

This task should be presented as one component in the context of a larger unit on this topic.

Building Understanding

As a class, brainstorm a list of foods that are processed in both the developing countries and the developed countries you have targeted for this activity. Organize students in pairs and have each pair select a food item to focus on. Within each pair, have the students locate and collect production data about the food they have selected for both a developed and a developing country.

Establish a list of categories for the data search. Some suggested categories include:

- Relevant health and safety regulations
- Types and purpose of chemicals used
- Equipment used for production and safety
- Age/training of workers
- Inspection methods
- Costs

Arrange time in the school library to work with the teacher librarian to help the students during this stage of the activity and to ensure that students use a wide variety of resources.

Ask the pairs of students to work together to sort the information they have gathered for both countries using the categories suggested above. Afterward, have them record their findings on the chart at the top of the *Making Comparisons* organizer on page 106. The focus question could be something like:*What effects do different food production methods have?* The topic columns could be labelled as something like: *Food production in <u>country name</u>.*

Next, instruct the students to identify the similarities and differences between the two countries. Have students use the Venn diagram on the organizer to help get an overview of the differences and to determine relationships based on both similarities and differences.

At this stage, students will require time for further investigation to discover the effects of the production methods and how these impact on various aspects of society. You might find it useful to use the *Investigating Effect* organizer on page 97 here. Remind students to revisit the list of categories established earlier. Have the pairs of students select a couple of categories that offer the most interesting data (either positive or negative) and record point-form information on the effects and the ultimate impact. These notes and those on the organizer will help them to make a personal reflection on the issues and serve as a basis for the report required in Demonstrating Understanding. After ample time to investigate, have students complete the reflection, *I think that ...* on the *Making Comparisons* organizer.

Demonstrating Understanding

In preparation for a mock summit on food production in developing countries, instruct each pair of students to prepare a report which identifies commendable practices for food production in developing countries.

Check It Out
For students who are interested in exploring related issues, we suggest *Iqbal Masih and the Crusaders Against Child Slavery* (Susan Kuklin, 1998) and *Free the Children* (Craig Kielburger and Kevin Major, 1998).

Exploring Questions about Text

Info Task
Students explore questions to help them process information.

Clarifying the Task

In order for students to learn to be active readers, writers and researchers, they need to learn a process for approaching text. In this task they learn how to get an overview, make some predictions, read for meaning and clarify understanding by exploring questions about the text.

Building Understanding

Instruct students to scan a selection of text from an article, textbook, reference book, electronic site, database, Internet, or encyclopedia. Introduce students to the *think, pair, share* strategy:

- Think — think about the text you have scanned
- Pair — tell a partner what you predict the focus of the text is
- Share — share ideas with the class and then discuss them

Ask students to next read the assigned text. You may need to adapt this strategy for students who are not reading at the level of the selected passage. For example, assign a group of students to read the passage aloud so everyone is included.

After completing the reading, have students work with the organizer *Prompts to Build Understanding* on page 107 as a guide to help them design probing questions about the content of the text. Remind students that they should be creating questions that will prompt analysis of the passage.

Have students select four questions that they think will really inspire someone to think critically about the text. Instruct students to record their four questions on an index card. Designate two corners of your room as "Bear Pits." Explain to your class that they will be able to pose their questions to other students in a Bear Pit, as well as respond to the questions of others. Assign three students at a time to each of the two Bear Pits and encourage everyone to pose their questions and try to answer their peers' questions. Provide ample time for this process. Afterward, have students return to their seats and answer their own questions.

Demonstrating Understanding

Arrange seating in a circle and hold a round-table discussion with your students. Instruct students to think about:

- What worked and why?
- What didn't work for them and why?
- How can they make the strategy better for everyone next time?
- How can they use this strategy for other purposes (e.g., analyzing literature, poetry, art, music)?

Check It Out
For detailed information and lots of lesson ideas relating to teaching the skill of questioning see *Asking Better Questions* (Morgan and Saxton, 1994).

Responding to Text

Info Task
Students discover how the Women's Movement has contributed to current North American society through responding to a chosen text.

Clarifying the Task

This task should be presented as one activity in the context of a unit on the Women's Movement. In the task, students learn how to analyze an information piece by reacting to the information on a personal level and then, through collaboration with others, further developing their understanding and reaching consensus as a group.

Building Understanding

Select a chapter or portion of a history text pertaining to the Women's Movement that you want students to analyze and respond to. Ensure that students have sufficient background on the topic to be able to understand the content of the passage.

Ask students to read the selection. Remind them of the skills involved in active reading. You may need to provide students with "active reader prompts" such as:

- Determine the main idea
- Identify supporting information and important points
- Make connections
- Make mental pictures

Give students large adhesive notes or index cards so they can do some "elbow thinking," and record questions, comments and concerns as they are reading. Make sure students understand that elbow thinking requires them to react to the text in an informal way only (i.e., jotting down feelings, ideas, questions, connections, etc.).

Afterward, provide students with reflection time. Have them close their text and record a visual (e.g., drawing, graffiti, cartoon, design, etc.) interpretation of the reading selection. Remind students to refer to their elbow thinking record.

Demonstrating Understanding

Create small groups of three or four students. Ask students to share their visual responses and to explain what they represent and why. Have each student record the key data, information and ideas in point form on the organizer *Group Response to Text* on page 108.

When everyone has shared, have students look for common understandings and record them in the box in the center of the organizer. Share these common understandings with the other groups and discuss to confirm that desired learning has been met. Consider:

- Was there consensus on the contributions?
- Did any group determine something unique?
- Were students able to substantiate their conclusions?

Check It Out
It is important to provide students with opportunities to build understanding using different strengths and intelligences. For ideas, see *Multiple Intelligences: The Theory in Practice* (Howard Gardner, 1995).

Interpreting Non-Fiction Text

Info Task

Students work in information circles to learn how to interpret non-fiction text about who lived in early pioneer villages and settlements and what contributions these settlers made to their communities.

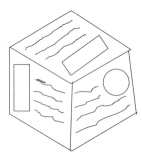

Information Cube

Check It Out

To discover more about conducting literature circles, see *Literature Circles* (Harvey Daniels, 1994).

Clarifying the Task

Information circles work on the same principle as literature circles, only in this case the students read non-fiction instead of fiction. Before implementing information circles, teach the roles and give students lots of experience responding to text using the role strategies so they are able to change roles without too much assistance. Consider appointing a student in each group to be responsible for keeping everyone on task.

Building Understanding

Guide students to select relevant, non-fiction books on pioneer life from the school library that are at an appropriate reading level. Explain that they will work in groups of four or five to explore their books for a week, taking turns in different "Information Circle" roles as the week progresses.

To introduce the roles, hand out the job description organizers on pages 109 to 113 — *Data Digger, Illustrator, Questioner, Reflector* and *Wordsmith* — which define the different roles and provide an "organizer" section for recording their discoveries. Also, provide the students with folders to keep all of their information organized. The roles are as follows:

- *Data Digger* — Your job is to read a section of your book and find fascinating bits of information. Jot down these gems on your organizer and record why this data is important. Prepare to share with your group.
- *Illustrator* — Your job is to read a section of your book and decide how you can share the information you have discovered using an illustration. It can be a picture, cartoon, labeled sketch, graph, etc. Prepare to share with your group.
- *Questioner* — Your job is to skim through your book and read pictures, graphics, headlines and subtitles. As you are skimming, jot down questions you have about things you are discovering. Put adhesive notes on the pages you have questions about so you can find them quickly when you are sharing with your group.
- *Reflector* — Read a section in your book. Use the reflection prompts on your organizer to help you make connections to your new discoveries. Prepare to share with your group.
- *Wordsmith* — Your job is to read a section of your book. As you read, watch for new and interesting words and phrases. Record these words and phrases, as well as what you think they mean. Use a dictionary to make sure you have the correct meaning. Plan to share your words and phrases with the group.

Demonstrating Understanding

Have each group create an "Information Cube" to synthesize and share their learning with the other groups. To do this, students create a large cube and use the six sides to present their information. The information should include text, as well as a variety of visuals. Encourage students to use visual media techniques to make their Information Cubes effective. Display the cubes to build a wall of new learning.

Interpreting Primary Sources

Info Task

Students interpret information from primary sources to discover who World War I affected and how the war impacted on these groups/individuals.

Clarifying the Task

Interpretation of primary sources requires a specialized set of skills. In this task, students are asked to demonstrate an understanding of the impact of World War I on the world community. In order to acquire the understanding, students learn how to analyze a primary source, discuss it, and record their interpretations of it.

Building Understanding

Collect primary sources such as diary entries, posters, video footage and artifacts. Ensure that a range of perspectives is covered by the sources (e.g., soldiers', politicians', wives', children's, etc.). Many books and Internet sites have copies of primary documents. As well, contact local community individuals and organizations to locate authentic primary sources where possible. Make sure students understand what a primary source is before commencing.

Place each primary source on a large chart-paper pad on a table. Divide students into small work groups, one group per source. Instruct each group to study its source (e.g., read, view, touch, etc.) to discover answers to questions such as:

- Who was affected by the war?
- What was the effect?
- Was the effect direct or indirect?

Ask the students to discuss their findings. After the discussion, direct students to individually record on the chart paper the thoughts, responses or questions that they have.

On a signal, ask students to move to another table, read the responses of the previous group and add their own thoughts. Continue the learning carousel until all groups have returned to their original table. On returning to their home group table, ask the students to read and discuss the comments on their chart.

While students are talking, circulate and facilitate discussion as required. Watch for indicators of success such as:

- Are all students involved in the discussion?
- Do thoughts, questions and remarks indicate that students understand the task?
- Are students beginning to relate to the impact the war had on some of the people being discussed?
- Are students able to empathize with different groups impacted by the war?
- Are they identifying positive as well as negative effects?
- Are the discoveries prompting thought resulting in further questions?

Demonstrating Understanding

Have individual students write a response in an appropriate role (e.g., soldier, parent, wife, politician, etc.) for the primary source their group was working on. Consider whether written responses indicate an understanding of the impact of the war on the particular individual(s).

Check It Out

Drama is a powerful strategy to help students synthesize their understanding of complex issues. If students have prerequisite drama skills, instruct each group to create a freeze tableau of the moment in time when a photograph was taken, diary entry was made, quotation was delivered, etc. Share tableaux and debrief.

Analyzing Visual Information

Info Task
Students analyze a photograph from a newspaper or periodical to discover implicit and explicit information messages.

Clarifying the Task

Visual information is often more powerful than printed text. In this task students learn how to analyze photographs to gain information.

Building Understanding

Group students in pairs. Provide each group with a photograph from a newspaper or magazine. As you select photos for this task, consider:

- Are the photos related to curriculum, or to current events in the community or world issues?
- Will students be familiar with the topic or do they need some background information?
- Do the photos have sufficient detail to provide students with triggers to spark critical thinking?
- Have students had experiences reading and analyzing newspaper and magazine articles?

Give students time to think about what they are viewing. Ask them to exchange a first reaction to the photo. Instruct them to discuss their reactions to the photograph in terms of explicit and implicit messages prompted by the photo. Provide students with reflection prompts that help them to think a little deeper and look a little deeper. For example:

- Who is in the picture?
- Where is the picture taken?
- When was the picture taken?
- What might have just happened?
- What happened just before the photographer took the picture?
- What might happen next?
- Who else is involved/concerned? Why?
- How will people react to this photo? Why?

Have students draft a short news story to go with the photo. Instruct them to review the first draft, edit and rewrite. Ask students to create a catchy title for the article and a photo caption to capture the readers' attention. Remind students to think and write like a reporter. Explain that they should include details of the event, quotes from people interviewed on location, data from research and opinions from "experts." As well, review the report writing format, particularly the importance of strong beginning and ending paragraphs. Post the photos and corresponding news stories on a bulletin board for sharing.

Demonstrating Understanding

Hold a sharing circle. Invite students to share:

- Discoveries about reading pictures to gain information
- Observations about the skills a news reporter needs
- Personal challenges during the assignment

Continue to provide other opportunities for students to read and analyze photographs, illustrations, graphs and charts to gain information.

Check It Out
To find out more about the importance of visual information see *Nonfiction Matters* (Stephanie Harvey, 1998) and *I See What You Mean* (Steve Moline, 1996).

Analyzing Media

Info Task
Students analyze an editorial cartoon to discover the techniques used to express ideas in this media format.

Clarifying the Task

Editorial cartoons are a unique and powerful media format. Through an examination of these cartoons, students can apply critical analysis skills that include responding personally and building on the responses of others. It is helpful to know if students have had prior experience deconstructing media or if this is a first experience.

Building Understanding

Collect editorial cartoons from a variety of newspapers and magazines. You will need one cartoon for every three or four students. Select cartoons that students will be able to connect with. For example, you may wish to link this experience with current events or a curriculum topic you are exploring. Mount each cartoon in the middle of a large sheet of paper.

Group students and assign a cartoon to each group. Invite students to analyze and discuss the cartoon. Provide students with analysis prompts or elicit the critical thinking prompts from students. Here are a few to get you started:

> • Whose point of view is this?
> • Who or what will this cartoon influence?
> • Whose perspective is missing?
> • What might you infer from this work?
> • How do you feel about it? Why?
> • Do others feel differently? Why?
> • How does the cartoonist make use of exaggeration, appeal to emotion, etc?

Afterward, ask each student to respond to the cartoon with words, sketches, questions, comments, etc. to form a group graffiti response. Have the groups leave one student at their table as a "docent" to explain the home group reaction. Direct the rest of the students to move to another table to add their responses to those already recorded. Continue the graffiti carousel as long as time permits. Post responses for sharing. Consider whether students have understood the cartoonist's message in their responses.

Demonstrating Understanding

Ask each student to create a cartoon which represents his/her point of view about a local school or community issue and to record a reflective rationale for his/her visual representation. Consider whether students are able to transfer their understanding of what cartoonists do to the creation of their own cartoon. Post cartoons and reflections for sharing.

Check It Out

Subscribe to a local newspaper for classroom use. Newspapers provide a wealth of current information that is readily accessible to students. Articles, editorials, ads and photographs give students authentic experiences with information text and provide models for their own demonstrations of learning.

Interpreting Spin

Info Task

Students investigate a current controversial issue or event and interpret its spin.

Clarifying the Task

Controversial issues hit the news daily. Usually we initially hear something that is fairly factual, but within hours all the groups who have an interest in the topic have had their "spin doctors" manipulate the information to present their slant on it. Before long, no one is clear what the facts really are. In this task, students learn how to recognize spin, identify the parties doing the spinning, and interpret their goals/intentions.

Building Understanding

Select a current issue that is controversial and engaging for your students (e.g., a bid to host the Olympic games, a housing development on a greenbelt, etc.). Work as a class to:

- Define the issue/event clearly and briefly.
- List the basic facts that all parties acknowledge: What really happened/will happen? When? Where? How? (e.g., Olympics will require transportation systems, housing, money, etc.).
- Identify the "sides" and label them A, B, C ... (e.g., businesses, activists, politicians, taxpayers, athletes, etc.).
- Identify the intention of each side: Who does each side want to convince and of what? What is the ultimate goal of each group?
- What do they hope to gain?

Record this information on the *Spin* organizer on page 114 using an LCD display panel or acetate on an overhead projector. Work together to note the spin/slant/version of one side and the counterspins. Divide the class into small groups and give them lots of time to discuss the information they have compiled.

Prompt them to compare the facts with spins, and the spins with counterspins. Encourage students to extrapolate when considering the comments from each side. Explain that they should think about effect, impact, ripple effects, future impact, etc. (see Info Tasks on these topics). Make sure that they consider these facets of the issue from all sides. For example: What if a city wins the right to host the games/what if it doesn't?

Demonstrating Understanding

Select a related issue (e.g., funding for training of potential Olympic athletes) and have the students apply this process working in small groups, and using a paper or electronic version of the *Spin* organizer. Organize an activity simulating a town hall meeting or television/radio talk show where people participate via e-mail, phone or using a microphone in the hall. Divide students into groups representing those identified during the exercise and have them participate in role. Follow the issue and discuss it as it develops over time.

Check It Out

Have the students watch some of the "spin" programs on local television (e.g., call-in shows, e-mail-in shows, political debates, etc.) to help them prepare for this task.

Determining Influence

Info Task

Students investigate marketing and advertising to discover how these forms of information influence the food choices of teenagers.

Clarifying the Task

Our students live in a world dominated by corporate advertising. This task can help students develop critical analysis skills in regard to ads. After going through a process to determine how much influence commercial advertising has on the food choices of teens, they examine the techniques used by advertisers and the influence these techniques have on teens. Students collect the necessary data from both primary and secondary sources.

Building Understanding

Review advertising strategies using a video such as *Why Ads Work* or *The Learning Seed*. Discuss how these tactics are used in food ads (e.g., animation, famous people, popular music, color, etc.).

Brainstorm food ads and promotions (print, audio and audiovisual) aimed at teenagers. Over several days, have students work in small groups to locate ads and note the characteristics of each. Students should visit their school library to seek Web sites and consult print materials about commercial advertising. You may need to suggest sources of advertising to ensure that students are exposed to a wide variety of formats and types of marketing techniques. They need to be aware not only of the techniques used to sway teen choices, but also the messages and values the advertising promotes.

Using this information, ask student groups to create a questionnaire to collect data on teen food choices and teen reactions to ads and promotions. Their questions need to get at the direct effects the advertising has on teens (e.g., feelings, purchasing habits, consuming practices and image). If students have never conducted surveys before, see the Info Task *Designing Surveys* on page 45. Have each student conduct interviews with a set number of different teens to complete the questionnaire.

Ask the groups to tally their results and then collate their findings with the rest of the class on a master organizer or in a simple database. To help students analyze their survey results and determine the influence advertising has on teen food choices, encourage them to use the organizer *Drawing Conclusions* on page 115.

Demonstrating Understanding

Have the students individually hypothesize on why teens react the way they do to the ads and promotions for food and prepare a brief summary of their findings. In small groups, ask students to share their summaries. Give each group a large piece of chart paper and instruct them to list the concerns they have as a result of this task and some actions they could take as individuals or as a group to combat the influence of advertising on teen food choices.

Check It Out

To investigate what teenagers really should be eating, log on to Web sites such as: http://www.schoolfile.com/nutrition.htm.

Developing a Point of View

Info Task
Students investigate technological innovations related to sound energy to develop a point of view on how these innovations have brought about changes in quality of life.

Clarifying the Task

Students cannot develop a point of view on global issues unless they have been exposed to a reasonable amount of information about a topic. To prepare students for this task, you will need to arrange a variety of exploratory activities on technological innovations related to sound energy. These will help students gain an overview of the breadth of the topic and a range of perspectives on the issues.

Building Understanding

Consider using some of the following resources and strategies to help students build background information on technological innovations related to sound energy:

- Video clips
- Newspapers and magazines
- Books and the Internet
- Excursion to a shopping center
- Guest speaker
- Displays and artifacts organized by students
- Brainstorming
- Questioning
- Discussions

After the exploratory activities, ask each student to select a technological innovation related to sound energy that is of interest to them (e.g., telephone, hearing aid, electric guitar, baby monitor, cell phone, etc.). Have the students research the technology they have selected and the impact that technology has had on quality of life. For ideas on helping students to discover impact, see the Info Task *Discovering Impact* on page 50. You will need to discuss the term "quality of life" with your students.

Work with the teacher librarian to plan the exploration activities and set students up for their individual research. Remind students to also investigate experts, associations, organizations, museums, etc. Provide students with prompts from the organizer *Pondering Perspective* on page 120 and remind them to examine the issue from a variety of perspectives. This will help them to develop their own point of view on the topic.

Have students record their discoveries on the organizer *My Point of View* on page 116. This organizer will prompt students to analyze the data they are gathering and to think about the reasons for their reactions. The reflective stems on the organizer will help students synthesize their information, and guide them through the thought processes involved in developing a point of view.

Demonstrating Understanding

Have students work in groups to share their personal point of view about the particular technology they researched and its impact. Students need to bring their organizer to the table to share with the group how and why they developed their personal point of view. Have each student complete the learning log *Thinking about Understanding* on page 117.

Check It Out
Your students can benefit from experiences with examining literature to determine point of view. Review the concept by reading and discussing two or three picture books on a similar topic but from different viewpoints (e.g., *The Three Little Pigs* [a classic version] and *The True Story of the 3 Little Pigs by A. Wolf* [Jon Scieszka, 1989]).

Forming an Opinion

Clarifying the Task

In this task, students learn that developing an opinion is a process. The students first identify those who already have a point of view on a chosen environmental issue such as the Grand Banks fishing rights issue, and then proceed to gather facts and opinions. They then develop understanding and form a personal opinion on the issue as they work through several individual and collaborative activities.

Building Understanding

Introduce your chosen topic with a short video clip to give an overview of some of the issues. Provide your students with a question to focus this part of the task (e.g., Should fishing rights on the Grand Banks be restricted?). Discuss the question and the issues.

Collaboratively generate a list of stakeholders and perspectives for the students to investigate. Have students individually explore a variety of sources and record each relevant idea or piece of information they discover on small cards or adhesive notes. Remind students that they need to examine the topic from a variety of perspectives using a variety of resources (e.g., a factual book, an environmental Web site, an article addressing the issues, etc.). Ask students to sort the facts and ideas they record into three columns (Agree, Disagree, Not sure).

Have students share their analysis with two or three other students and discuss varying points of view. At this point, encourage individual students to process their thinking in a learning log entry that will prompt them to generate an opinion based on their personal analysis of the viewpoints and information they have gathered. The learning log entry should include the following:

• Focus Question: _____
• I discovered that _____
• I wonder why _____
• What if _____
• I believe that _____
• In my opinion _____

Demonstrating Understanding

Have students work from their learning logs to prepare a brief presentation. Ask students to present and defend their analysis and opinions in a mock public forum. They must be prepared to field questions and challenges.

To ensure student success:

- Decide on the criteria for assessment of the process and the presentation.
- Create an assessment tool and share it with the students.
- Set ground rules for the forum (e.g., questions and challenges should be constructive).
- Videotape the presentations so students can review them and set goals for improvement.

Making Judgments about Issues

Info Task

Students research events, inventions and discoveries related to space exploration in order to make a personal judgment about the impact of space exploration.

Clarifying the Task

In order to make judgments on this topic, students need to identify the events and discoveries in space exploration and the significance of those discoveries. This task would be most successful as one component of a much larger unit on space. The task itself provides a processing framework for students to analyze and synthesize complex issues.

Building Understanding

After students have had preliminary experiences on the topic of space exploration, they need opportunities to link their prior learning to the current inquiry.

Individual research should begin in the school library in partnership with the teacher librarian. Together you need to think about how well your students are prepared for independent research. Consider:

- What do they already know?
- What do they need to find out?
- Where can they find information to meet their needs?
- What keywords can they use to maximize their searching potential?

Encourage students to use a variety of resources and to seek out all possible perspectives on the issue.

Provide students with the organizer *Making Judgments* on page 118 to record and analyze their data. Upon completion, instruct students to create a collaborative timeline of events/discoveries related to space exploration. Have students add the benefits and drawbacks of each event/discovery. Use different colors of paper or markers for visual impact when recording benefits and drawbacks.

Demonstrating Understanding

Ask students to examine the information on the timeline in order to make a personal judgment about the overall impact of space exploration on the quality of human life, and to record this in their learning log. You may wish to provide your students with another visual organizer such as a PMI (Pluses, Minuses, Interesting) chart to organize their thinking through this phase of synthesis. Remind students to explore all perspectives and both positive and negative opinions as they work to develop their own personal judgment about the impact of space exploration. Invite students to share and defend their judgment in discussion groups.

Check It Out

Current topics such as this one require students to have access to up-to-date information. Direct them to some of the many NASA Web sites. For example:

- http://spacelink.nasa.gov/
- http://arc.nasa.gov/
- http://kids.msfc.nasa.gov/

Making Judgments about Media

Info Task
Students review a video and make a judgment about its suitability for use with other students.

Clarifying the Task

Media, such as video, is a construct. Students need to know the techniques that are used by the industry to produce effective video (e.g., sound track, appeals to emotion). By providing students with an authentic opportunity to view and critique a video on a chosen curriculum topic, they are able to develop specific skills for dealing with video as an information source.

Building Understanding

In small groups, ask students to view selected videos. Each group will need to work with a different one. Remind students to use video as they would print text. For example, encourage them to rewind and fast forward on the video machine in order to review and analyze certain segments of the video.

Have students work individually, using the organizer *Media Analysis* on page 119 to deconstruct their video and begin to form an opinion about its suitability as an information piece to show to another class or classes. As they work, watch to see whether students are able to identify the characteristics and needs of the class(es) the video is being considered for.

Demonstrating Understanding

Ask each student to write a short review of their video and publish it to share with the class. Encourage them to include the following elements:

- Short summary of content
- Content effectiveness
- Content accuracy and validity
- Technical effectiveness
- Personal opinions and judgment on suitability

In looking at the reviews, consider:

- Have students identified both the technical and content elements of the production and commented on their effectiveness?
- Have students been able to succinctly summarize the video content?
- Have students examined the validity of the information presented by looking at the producer's credibility, and the intent, currency and accuracy of the information?
- Have students considered the characteristics and needs of the class(es) the video is being selected for?
- Have students presented an informed opinion and defended it?
- Have students made a judgment about the suitability of the video?

Check It Out
Visit *Media Awareness Network* at http://www.media-awareness.ca/ to discover many other media tasks for students.

Making Decisions

Info Task

Students recall and collect information on the care of pets to make an informed decision about which animal might make a good pet for a classroom.

Clarifying the Task

In this task, students relate prior learning to a new information inquiry. They use information from their research about pets to make an informed decision about choosing a classroom pet.

Building Understanding

Read a story to the students about a child and his/her pet. Discuss their reactions to the story. Afterward, do a survey with the class. Ask questions such as:

- Who has a pet at home?
- What kind of pet is it?
- Who has a friend who has a pet?

Tally the results of the survey and create a visual representation (e.g., bar graph, pictograph, etc.).

As well, ask students to draw pictures of themselves or their friends caring for a pet. Share the drawings in small groups and discuss the needs and care for various pets. Encourage all students to participate in the discussion. Share findings and record them in the "Know" column of a KNL chart. If a KNL chart is new to students, you will need to model what the headings mean: *Know, Need to Know* and *Learned.*

When this is done, ask the students to return to their small groups and identify and discuss characteristics that might be important for a classroom pet. During the discussion, consider:

- Are the children without pets joining in?
- If not, what can be done to entice them?

Encourage the groups to articulate questions they still have about pets they are considering. Share these and add them to the "Need to Know" column of the KNL chart. For example:

- How much space does the pet need?
- How often does the pet need to be fed?
- When does the pet sleep?

Arrange time for groups to work with the teacher librarian in the school library to find the answers to their questions.

When most of the answers have been discovered, collaboratively review the findings and develop a list of desirable characteristics for a classroom pet.

Demonstrating Understanding

Ask each student to complete a reflection and make a recommendation for a classroom pet. The reflection might look like this:

How to Choose a Pet for the Classroom

Three important things:
   A classroom pet must
   -
   -
   -
I think our new pet should be a _____ because_____.

Afterwards, tabulate the results and hope for the best!

Check It Out

Share a video with students on the care of pets. This experience will help students to recall prior knowledge and provide a common vocabulary.

Exploring Solutions

Students explore solutions for a situation that is potentially dangerous to personal safety by determining how to seek appropriate assistance.

Clarifying the Task

This task helps students develop the knowledge and skills required for making informed decisions when dealing with potentially dangerous situations. Students learn how to break down a problem, look for relationships among the parts, and collaboratively explore solutions.

Building Understanding

Ask students to collect news stories about teens involved in dangerous situations. Share these stories, discuss them, and make a list of potentially dangerous situations (e.g., smoking, drinking and driving, using firearms, etc.).

Have students work in pairs to select a situation and to investigate it to discover details. Ask them to record their data and to prepare to analyze it by identifying relationships. Instruct students to organize their information on a web, either by drawing a web by hand or by using a computer application. This web can help them to explore the predetermined relationships.

Direct the students to identify possible people, organizations, support groups, equipment and strategies they might use to determine solutions for seeking appropriate assistance. Establish criteria for predicting the success of the suggested strategies (e.g., speed, realism, effectiveness, impact, availability, etc.).

Finally, ask students to share the details of their situation, their analysis and possible solutions. Provide them with a cross-classification chart such as the one shown here to use so that they can evaluate the usefulness of each strategy in terms of the suggested criteria (e.g., speed, realism, effectiveness, impact, availability, etc.).

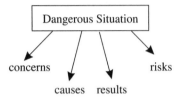

Strategy

Criteria

Rating

Demonstrating Understanding

Instruct student groups to select a dangerous situation and to create a skit that illustrates the danger and the strategies students could apply to reduce the danger or obtain assistance. The skit should demonstrate their application of the previously established criteria. Debrief immediately following each skit.

Collect a variety of related flyers, pamphlets, posters, etc. from agencies, support groups and organizations and make them available for students.

Synthesizing Findings

Info Task

Students assess the impact of the use and disposal of various products on the environment and synthesize their findings to suggest possible solutions.

Clarifying the Task

In this task students are given prompts to help them explore all perspectives of an issue and a graphic organizer to assist them to build personal meaning. The students then use this information to help them see possible solutions to problems they uncovered.

Building Understanding

Ask students to keep track of items they see people throwing in the garbage that concern them as future stewards of the environment. Have students share their lists of products where the use and disposal is controversial (e.g., plastic soda pop containers, broken appliances, etc.). Discuss the typical issues surrounding some of the products, such as uses, manufacturing processes, longevity and alternative uses.

Have each student select a product to research. Familiarize students with the organizer *Pondering Perspective/Investigating Impact* on page 120. Instruct students to use the prompts on this organizer to scaffold their thinking and to help them cover all the relevant considerations as they are selecting resources and discovering information about their product. Remind students to keep going back to *Pondering Perspective* as they conduct their research to make sure they are considering all relevant points of view.

Once students have gathered their data, provide them with direction to help them develop a personal hypothesis about the impact of the product on the environment. Have students record this hypothesis, along with supporting evidence and conflicting opinions, using *Synthesizing — Making New Meaning* on page 121. In the "New Ideas" section, have students record new, personal, innovative suggestions for dealing with any problems identified. Encourage students to consider questions such as:

- What does this information really mean?
- What impact does it have?
- How do I feel about it today? How will I feel about it in ten years?

The following is an example of a hypothesis and suggestions for new ideas for the inquiry question: How do pleasure power boats affect the environment?

- Hypothesis: I believe that even though powerboats provide a lot of fun for the users, they bother people and animals and pollute the water.
- New Ideas: Establish some quiet lakes where only watercraft without motors are allowed.

Demonstrating Understanding

This is an opportune time to initiate an interactive activity to give students an opportunity to test out their ideas with their peers. See the Info Task *Clarifying Meaning* on page 41 for a possible activity. Organize a mock press conference, similar to the one in the Info Task *Considering Alternatives* on page 51, for students to present their suggestions and respond to questions and challenges.

Check It Out

Many students will choose topics related to the disposal of products. They will require up-to-date information on local regulations related to recycling and disposing of products. Check the pamphlets and Web sites of local government and environmental associations.

Relating Findings

Info Task

Students study a current environmental crisis and relate their findings to similar occurrences to determine what should be done to eliminate such a crisis in the future.

Clarifying the Task

This is an issues-related task. Students need to first investigate an environmental crisis, like a recent oil spill, to determine cause and effect. They then relate their findings to similar situations and the suggestions of others before making recommendations for changes to eliminate this sort of problem.

Building Understanding

Arrange time for students to access a variety of relevant information sources in the school library on a recent environmental crisis. Because of the current nature of this information task, your students will need to search on-line databases and the Internet to acquire up-to-date articles. Students will need a tool for evaluating Web sites and validating sources. See *Check It Out* for suggestions.

Have students create a graphic organizer (or provide one) to help them collect and sort information focused on the causes and effects of this crisis.
For example:

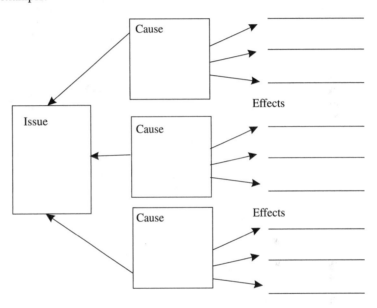

Next, instruct students to investigate similar situations to discover the recommendations, policy changes, laws and ideas of others. Using this information, and working in small groups, ask students to relate their findings to the current crisis and to suggest regulations and conditions that could prevent this disaster from occurring again.

Demonstrating Understanding

Have each group summarize its recommendations and present them to a mock hearing of a board, like the International Shipping Board, for consideration in the updating of regulations. Remind students that the recommendations must be feasible and that there must be logical connections between the causes and the recommendations. They must also articulate their reasons for each suggestion. In preparation for their presentations, ask students to think about guidelines a board might use to determine which recommendations to accept and implement.

Check It Out

Take a look at these Web sites for more ideas:
- Kathy Schrock's Guide for Educators:
  http://school.discovery.com/schrockguide/index.html
- Debbie Abilock Curriculum Site:
  http://nuevaschool.org/~debbie/library/overview.html

CHAPTER FIVE

Design for Success

We hope that *Info Tasks* is the beginning of a journey of discovery for teachers. Designing effective information tasks is a complex process that requires ongoing adjustments and refinements. In this book we have concentrated on only one segment of information literacy skills—those needed for processing. We urge teachers to check out our other publications which provide many detailed strategies and tools for helping students develop the full spectrum of information literacy skills. In the *Check It Out* sections of each task we have suggested links to many other rich resources that will help teachers build a wide repertoire of teaching and learning activities.

The information explosion is not about to end. Technology advances have changed the very notion of what information is. We have no idea what wizardry we are yet to experience in telecommunications, research and development, and explorations of other unknown frontiers. Teachers and students will have to continue to adapt to the evolution of information and changing technologies.

One constant is the desire of teachers to help students achieve their personal potential. To do this, we need to ensure that they have the skills and knowledge essential for helping them to understand their world and their role in shaping the future. It is through information tasks, such as those provided in this book, that we give students real-world opportunities to prepare for their own future. The "information" base for activities may be subject content or current issues/events related to curriculum. Information skills are not an addition to the ever-expanding curriculum, but the questioning, evaluating, analyzing and synthesizing skills that have always been essential for developing knowledge and for learning. The current and ever-increasing proliferation of information makes these skills crucial if students are to understand the relevance of what they are learning and be successful.

Often a student's reaction to an assignment that requires only recall and regurgitation of information is "So what?" Students tend to ask, "Now that I have collected all this stuff, what do I do with it?/Why did I have to do this?/What does it mean to me?" One can hardly blame them, as there is no apparent relevance or purpose for them. When students are required to process data and are provided with strategies and tools, such as those in the info tasks, to help them evaluate, sort, test, analyze and synthesize their information, then they are prepared and inspired to create something new with it. It is through such a process that they develop personal knowledge and understanding. Learning experiences then become relevant for students and consequently there is the potential for making real gains in learning and achievement levels.

We hope that *Info Tasks* has provided teachers with many ideas that will be springboards for lots of other experiences for students. When you are planning to have students work with information you may choose to design a single activity, a research project, a performance task or perhaps a WebQuest. Whatever form the assignment takes, we hope that teachers will focus more attention on the processing stage. Students do not innately know what to do with the information they have gathered. If teachers do not provide a process and scaffolding at this stage to help students develop personal understanding and build knowledge, then the results will probably be disinterest and plagiarized reports.

Because WebQuests are becoming a popular tool for integrating learning experiences using the Internet, we have prepared a couple to demonstrate how the processing stage is so vital to the success of this form of information task. The sample WebQuests can be found on pages 79 and 80 at the end of the chapter, along with a list of key characteristics. In the original work of Bernie Dodge, who developed and refined this strategy, one of the critical attributes of a WebQuest is a description of the process the learners should go through. The WebQuests we have created build on the micro skills developed in some of the information tasks in this book.

We suggest that independent research/inquiry projects, performance tasks and WebQuests be used as culminating activities to allow students to demonstrate their learning by applying the skills and knowledge from previous experiences. These kinds of complex information tasks, if carefully crafted, will help students build personal understanding.

Information tasks of all types require:

✔ A well defined purpose
✔ Clear assessment criteria
✔ A relevant real world challenge
✔ Engaging resources and strategies
✔ Learning experiences that build on one another to enhance understanding
✔ Feedback to students throughout the process
✔ Opportunities to work collaboratively
✔ A repertoire of information literacy skills
✔ Access to a variety of resources
✔ Access to information technologies
✔ Scaffolding (e.g., visual organizers, prompts)
✔ Strategies to model reflective learning (e.g., journals, learning logs)
✔ Opportunities to demonstrate understanding
✔ Opportunities to self assess and set goals for improvement
✔ Collaboration with a teacher librarian/media specialist where possible

As teachers we have control of the classroom experience and consequently of the learning opportunities for our students. If we pay special attention to the above criteria for designing successful information tasks we will improve our capacity to enhance student achievement.

We must remember that we are not alone in our schools. We urge teachers to work with colleagues in their schools and boards during the information task design process. For example, the teacher librarian/media specialist in a school is an information specialist, and can be an excellent resource and collaborator. The school library is more than just a facility to book so students have access to information sources and technologies. The facility does provide physical access to information. However, a teacher librarian/media specialist can help your students achieve intellectual access to the information they discover. Together, you can design powerful learning experiences for your students, and teach and assess for student success.

The impact of this kind of programming has recently been documented in *How School Librarians Help Kids Achieve Standards: The Second Colorado Study* (Lance, Rodney, Hamilton-Penell, April 2000). The study states: *A central finding of this study is the importance of a collaborative approach to information literacy. Test scores rise in both elementary and middle schools as media specialists and teachers work together. In addition, scores also increase with the amount of time library media specialists spend as in-service trainers of other teachers, acquainting them with the rapidly changing world of information.* Where possible, take advantage of this valuable resource person to help you design and facilitate assignments that will prompt students to process information, make personal connections and develop understanding.

Use *Info Tasks* to help build reading, writing and research skills.

✔ Design for learning
✔ Design for success

WebQuest: Eat Me First

Setting

You have been hired by a successful health food store chain to research, develop and promote a new product to be featured at the opening of their newest store. This store will cater exclusively to the adolescent market. Your employer has given you the task of discovering and creating the product.

Task

Create an infomercial about a new health food product that you will test out on each of the adolescents you used for your initial on-line survey. Use a tool such as *I Movie*™ or *Hyperstudio*™ to create your infomercial. Design a feedback form to evaluate the response to this new health food product designed specifically to address their needs as primary consumers.

Process

1. Conduct an on-line survey with several adolescents. Before you start, review your notes on conducting effective surveys. Be sure to survey a large enough number of young people in order to obtain reliable data. Your mission is to discover what adolescents eat and why, as well as what kind of food products they would like to have but are currently not available on the market. Remember that good data on a survey results from carefully constructed questions. Make sure your questions will get at the information you require.

2. Sort and record the data you gather from the survey in a table. This will help you to analyze the frequency of requested foods.

3. Research and record the kinds of foods adolescents need to be active and healthy. You will need to discover why these foods are necessary.

4. Record and compare your data by using the organizer *Making Comparisons* on page 106 to help you discover the relationship between what adolescents want and what is good for them.

5. Use the foods recorded in the center of the Venn diagram to target your new product. Brainstorm some possible products based on these foods—ones that are popular but also healthy choices.

6. Select your best idea and create a name for your new product.

7. Conference with a colleague about your progress to date.

8. Reflect, rethink, revise, rework and decide on a product.

9. Research media techniques used by industry to persuade consumers to make purchases. You will need to examine the targeted market—the adolescent consumer—and be aware of regulations governing advertising.

10. Use a storyboard to plan the visuals and text for your infomercial.

11. Share your infomercial with your original target group and provide them with a feedback form so you will be able to assess their initial reactions to your new product idea.

Information Resources

- http://www.schoolfile.com
- http://www.media-awareness.ca/

Evaluation

You will be evaluated on how effectively you have been able to:

- Make comparisons and analyze your data about food choices of adolescents and what the experts say is good for them
- Process and transfer information and promotional media techniques to your infomercial

The *Processing Rubric* on page 105 will be used for this evaluation.

Conclusion

Now that you have experienced first-hand the power of target marketing, perhaps you would like to find out more about the influence of media on other consumer trends. Knowing more about a topic is empowering. How has this task helped you to become a wiser consumer?

WebQuest: What Is the Weakest Link?

Setting

Every day species are disappearing from the face of the earth. What are the circumstances that lead to animal endangerment and extinction? Is there anything that students can do to raise awareness of the growing plight of animal life threatened by natural or human causes?

Task

Work as part of a team to research a habitat of your choice and investigate the animal life. Prepare with your team to mount an awareness campaign about the most fragile species found in your habitat. Deliver the central message of the campaign in a jingle to be broadcast in various formats. Your task is to create the lyrics for the jingle.

Process

1. Conference with your group and decide on a habitat (e.g., forest, marine, polar, mountain, desert, etc.).
2. Work out a plan. Think about the focus for research, information sources and timelines. Draw up a schedule and assign tasks. Each member of your team will need to have responsibility for a specific animal classification. Remember to make good use of everyone's particular talents and strengths as you progress through this task.
3. Investigate the animal group in the habitat that you have been assigned (e.g., mammals, birds, insects, etc.). Remember to gather information from all relevant perspectives (e.g., environmentalists, industry, government, etc.).
4. Create an organizer so all group members can sort their discoveries as they record them. For example:

Animal	Food	Enemies	Other Concerns

5. Collaborate to prepare food chains and a web of the animals' lives in your habitat. Use a software program like *Inspiration*™ to develop your web. You might need to use the *Ranking Information* organizer on page 89 to help you work out the hierarchy of animal life in the food chains before you try to build your web.
6. Examine the concerns discovered in your initial investigation.
7. Highlight four or five animals your group feels are in the greatest danger of being declared threatened. Provide a rationale for your choices.
8. Log on to Web sites such as *The World Wildlife Association* and *Species at Risk* to discover what is published about endangerment of animals in your habitat. Try to confirm your findings here, or by reading about the topic or contacting wildlife experts.
9. As a group decide which animal(s) will be the focus of your awareness jingle. Consult your animal charts and food chain web, and then brainstorm ideas and concepts you want to include in the jingle.
10. Write your jingle and record a reading of it. Try out some techniques such as different voices and sound effects to make the reading more powerful. Play the recording over the school broadcast system. Explore other ways you can share your message with the broader community.

Information Resources

- Books and articles on animals and habitats—remember to develop a list of possible keywords first to make searching more efficient and effective
- http://www.worldwildlife.org
- www.eelink.net/EndSpp
- www.speciesatrisk.gc.ca
- www.wilderness.org

Evaluation

You will be graded on:
- Research skills
- Group work skills

The *Information Literacy Rubric* on page 10 and the organizer *Assessing Group Work Skills* on page 93 will be used for this evaluation.

Conclusion

This task provided an opportunity to discover that each species is a special link in the web of life. With your jingle you have started to become involved in action needed to preserve habitats and the biodiversity within those habitats. Follow some of the links from the suggested Web sites to discover what else you can do to promote good stewardship of our environment.

Key Characteristics of WebQuests

A WebQuest:

❏ Is designed to measure student achievement of key expectations

❏ Is carefully crafted to allow students to demonstrate significant skills and knowledge and to attain personal understanding

❏ Requires students to apply prior knowledge and skills and acquire new knowledge to complete the task

❏ Utilizes multiple assessors that evaluate the learning process, as well as the product/performance

❏ Is designed to be as "real world" as possible and provide students with an authentic audience

❏ Is a research/inquiry-oriented activity requiring students to apply information literacy skills

❏ Gives students opportunity to apply higher-level thinking skills

❏ Motivates and challenges students, but is realistic and attainable

❏ Is often collaborative and encourages students to develop teamwork skills, but also requires students to take ownership of their own learning

❏ Connects students to pre-defined resource sites on the Internet

❏ May direct students to other sources of information (e.g., books, experts)

❏ Can be short or long term in duration

❏ Sets the context for the task in an engaging **introduction**

❏ Invites students to participate in a realistic and interesting **task** or a compelling problem

❏ Provides links to a set of **information sources** needed to complete the task

❏ Describes the **process** the student needs to take to complete the task

❏ Is designed to break down the process into carefully planned steps to help the student build understanding

❏ Provides **guidance** in the form of question prompts, graphic organizers and other organizational tools

❏ Provides a check for understanding in the **conclusion** and sometimes offers ideas for further activity

For more information and complete templates for creating WebQuests, visit The *WebQuest Page* at http://edweb.sdsu.edu/webquest/webquest.html.

Organizers for Information Tasks

Linking to Facts and Opinions

name: _____

Topic: _____

Facts	My Questions	Opinions	My Reactions

Perhaps . . .

Detecting Inconsistencies

Name: _____

Validation Criteria	Source:	Source:
Accuracy • Up to date • Statistical data/facts • Opinions		
Authority How credible is the writer/producer? • Qualifications • Experience Who financed the work? • Corporation • Government agency • Special interest group		
Perspective Whose perspective is included? Whose voice is excluded?		
Slant/Intent What is the purpose? • Inform • Convince • Entertain • Question • Support		
Context What is the context of the piece? • Historical • Political • Environmental • Social • Fiction • Factual		
Evidence of Bias • Exaggeration • Prejudice • Inclusion/exclusion • Charged words • Overgeneralization • Opinion asserted as fact		
My Analysis		

Working with Information

Name: _____

- Establish your information need
- Collect the best resources
- Actively read, view, listen
- Select and record relevant information
- Rework information visually
- Think about it

Recording—point-form notes and data	**Seeing**—webs, graphs, sketches

Thinking
What does it mean?
Why is it important?

What's the Difference?

Name: _____

Today	Medieval Times	I think it was like this in Medieval Times because . . .

Information Webbing

name: _____

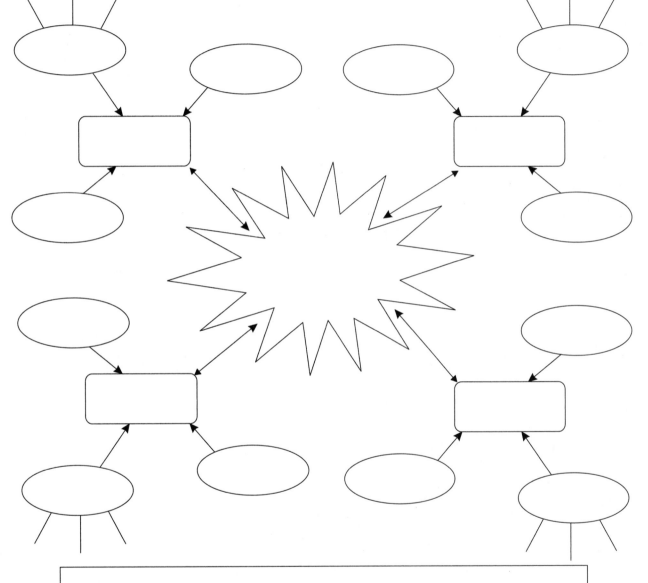

Thinking
What does this mean?
Why is it important?

Comparing Sources

Name: _____

Source: _____

Source: _____

Common Information

Source: _____

Ranking Information

name: _____

Focus Inquiry

Big Ideas

Supporting Information/Ideas

Data Evidence

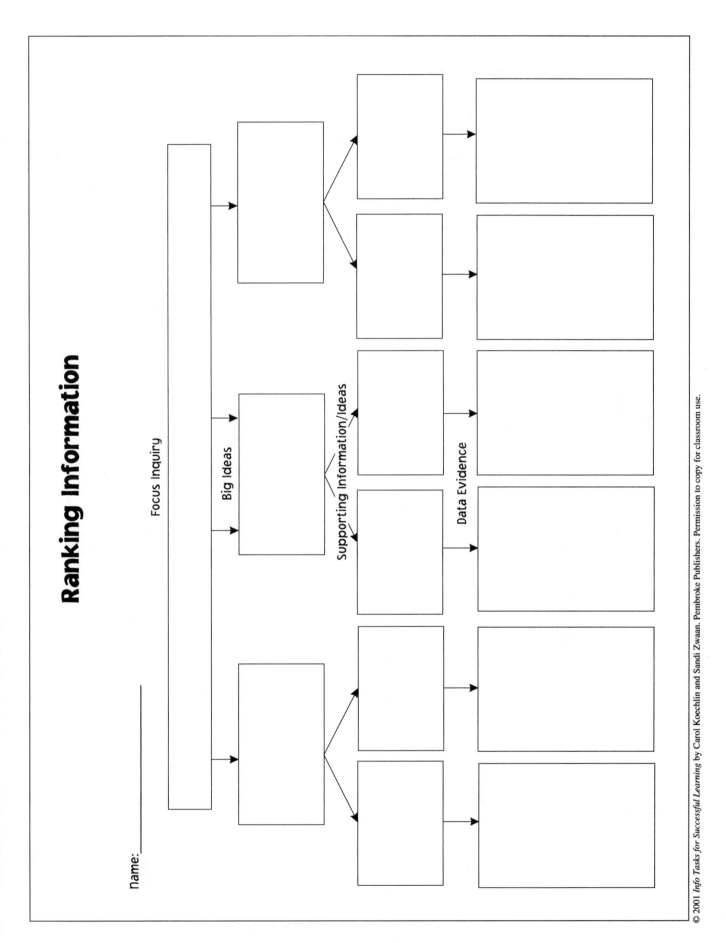

Topic Storming

Name: _____

What is my general topic? What am I specifically interested in? What am I curious about? What do I already know? What do I need to know?

Focus words: Which focus words will enrich my research question? Which focus words will help me analyze my data?

_____

Inquiry question/statement of purpose:

_____

_____

Sub-topics: Which sub-topics will help me organize my data? Predict categories you will need to explore.

- _____
- _____
- _____
- _____

Keywords:

changes, types, kinds, jobs, roles, importance, charac- teristics, structure, purpose, function, relation- ships, lifestyle, adaptations, conditions, defense, survival, compare, con- trast, cause, effect, value, significance, consequences, impact, infer, imply, project, analyze

Tips:
- Look for keywords in your "topic storming," sub-topics, indexes, table of contents
- Think about categories and classifications

Defining Information Needs

name: _____

Concerns/Questions	Exploration/Discoveries	Reflections

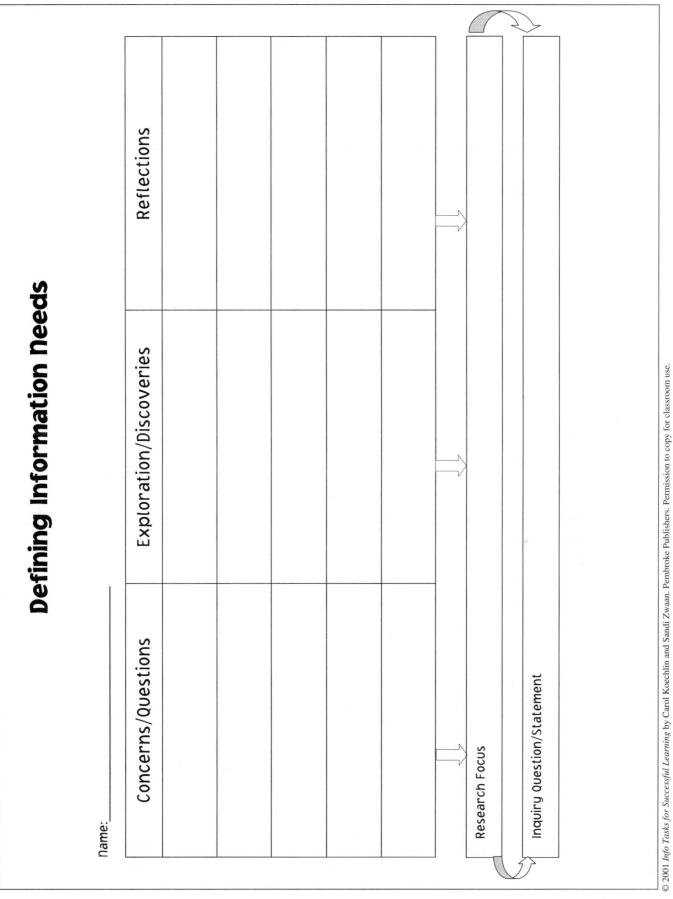

Research Focus

Inquiry Question/Statement

Questioning Rubric

Criteria	Level 1	Level 2	Level 3	Level 4
Focus	broad and unmanageable, or narrow with little scope	manageable, with limited exploration potential	will look at information from a variety of perspectives	will evoke personal reaction
Interest	of little personal interest	motivates some personal interest	stimulates curiosity and enthusiasm	inspires further investigation and more questions
Knowledge	requires lists, one word answers	requires collection of facts and opinions	directs personal reflection, opinion	catalyst for transfer or application
Processing	requires data collection only	requires classification of data	requires general comparison based on criteria	requires independent analysis, synthesis and application of information

Reprinted with permission from © Toronto District School Board

Assessing Group Work Skills

Name: _____

❑ We share ideas and information.
❑ We listen to each other without interruption.
❑ We show appreciation of each other.
❑ We encourage each other.
❑ We invite others to talk.
❑ We identify each other's strengths.
❑ We respond positively to new ideas.
❑ We make plans to complete work and stick to our agreements.
❑ We each accept responsibility for our tasks.
❑ We are open to the ideas of others.
❑ We seek other's opinions.
❑ We are aware of the feelings of everyone in our group.
❑ We are considerate of each other.
❑ We enjoy working together.

Our team could be stronger if:

_____
_____
_____
_____
_____

I think we should try to:

_____
_____
_____
_____
_____

During this task I discovered that working with others helped me because:

_____
_____
_____
_____
_____

Clarifying Understanding

Name: _____

Source: _____

Topic: _____

What I Want to Know	What I Found Out	Why it Is Important

I wonder if...

Consultation Process

Name: _____   Responding to: _____

My views	My needs

After Consultation	
New thoughts	More questions
Confirming viewpoints	Conflicting viewpoints

New understanding

Action!

Reacting to Media

Name: _____   Media title: _____

My Reactions	Thoughts/Questions
I was reminded of...	
I smiled when...	
I was worried when...	
I could imagine...	
I hoped...	
I thought about...	
It was like...	
I held my breath when...	
I was interested because...	
I was excited when...	
I would like to be...	
I'm glad I'm not...	
I would like...	
I wouldn't like...	
I would suggest...	

Investigating Effect

Name: _____

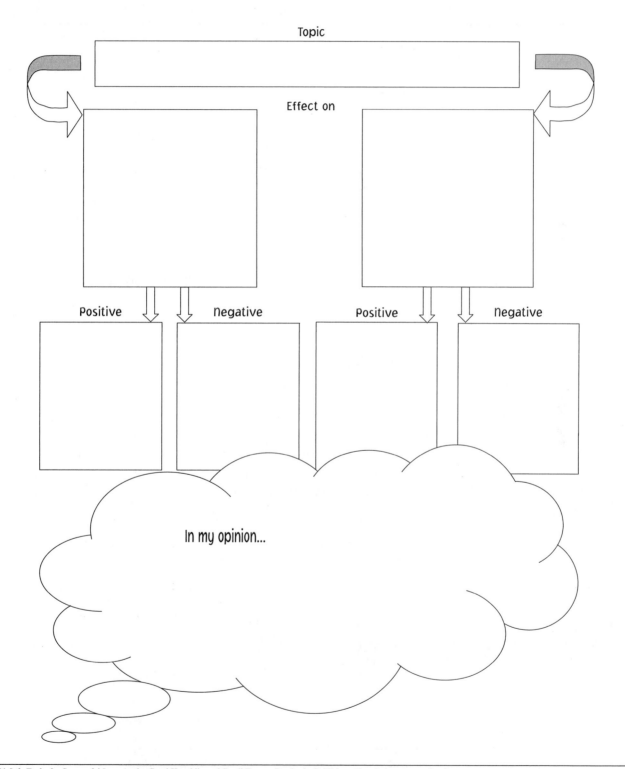

Topic

Effect on

Positive   Negative   Positive   Negative

In my opinion...

Determining Effect

Name: _____   Topic to be examined: _____

Plus +		because...
Minus —		because...
Questionable ?		because...
Aha !		This helps me understand...

Overall . . .

Discovering Impact

Name: _____   Topic:_____

Who/what was affected?	How?	What are the implications?

In view of this information...

Problems/Issues

Name: _____

Alternative idea + −	Alternative idea + −	Alternative idea + −
Possibly	Possibly	Possibly

Solutions to consider

Interpreting and Evaluating Graphs and Charts

Scan the graph/chart to get a quick overview. If it is effectively designed you should be able to gain all the necessary information quickly. Now read a little closer to interpret the graph/chart and evaluate its effectiveness.

What is the title?

What categories are represented?

What is the date of the study?

Can you tell how the data was collected?

Who produced the graph/chart?

Is there a key or legend? What does it tell you?

What visual techniques have been applied (color, texture, size)?

What does the graph/chart tell you?

Does it help you to understand the topic better? How?

Is there a better way of representing this information? If so, how and why?

Is there anything that you can detect that could possibly be misleading? Explain.

On the whole this graph/chart is/is not effective because...

Creation and Use of Graphic Organizers

Criteria	Level 1	Level 2	Level 3	Level 4
Use of graphic organizers	requires assistance to select an organizer	selects an existing organizer	adapts an existing organizer to a specific task	creates an effective graphic organizer for a specific task
Appropriateness of organizer	ineffective for this task	generic and useful but not specific to this task	task specific and relevant to defined need	task specific, facilitates thinking/analysis beyond defined need
Effectiveness of organizer	useful only for recording data	facilitates classifying and sorting of information	facilitates breakdown of information and seeing connections	facilitates higher level analysis of information (e.g., cause and effect, predicting, decision making)
Integration/transfer of computer skills/ software knowledge	selects and uses a ready-made organizer from available software	uses software to adapt an existing organizer	selects and uses appropriate software to create an organizer	innovative use of software, manipulates data dynamically (e.g., layering)

Reprinted with permission from © Toronto District School Board

Graphic Organizer Worksheet

Purpose
- Group/categorize
- Compare
- Question action or reaction
- Identify cause and effect
- Correlate data
- Dissect information
- Look for commonalties/discrepancies
- _____
- _____

Strategies to Try
- ☐ T charts
- ☐ Venn diagrams
- ☐ Webbing/mapping
- ☐ Arrows
- ☐ Shapes
- ☐ Color/shading
- ☐ _____
- ☐ _____

Sketches

Which organizer works best for my purpose?

_____

Why? _____

_____

Keeping Track of My Learning

Name: _____

Topic: _____

I think I did a good job...

It was difficult...

I enjoyed...

I wonder if...

I need work on...

I must remember...

Processing Rubric

Criteria	Level 1	Level 2	Level 3	Level 4
Concepts/ Reasoning	sorts data	orders and ranks data	classifies information and makes comparisons	experiments with information and uses it in different ways
Organizing	requires assistance to select an appropriate organizational strategy	independently selects an appropriate organizational strategy	able to modify a strategy/organizer for a specific task	creates effective organizers for a specific task
Communicating	accepts all data	evaluates data when prompted by teacher	applies teacher-suggested checks to evaluate data	systematically and regularly evaluates data for quality and quantity
Applying	retells findings	summarizes information	makes relationships and draws conclusions from information	independently applies knowledge to new and different situations

Making Comparisons

Name: _____   Focus question:_____

Topic _____	Topic _____

What is different or unique to this topic?	What is similar? What criteria/categories are you using to make comparisons?	What is different or unique to this topic?

I think that...

Prompts to Build Understanding

Now that you have gathered all this data you need to process it. That means you will have to **analyze** it — rework, reorganize, reread, reflect on the data you have gathered. It often helps to make use of graphic organizers that provide a visual interpretation for you. Try using these thinking prompts to spark links to your own thinking.

What is your information problem?

Is data reliable, accurate, up to date, biased...?

Identify different points of view.
      – How many are there?
      – Whose views are they?
      – Why does _____ believe _____?
      – Are there points of view missing? Whose?
      – Am I getting fact or opinion?

How is _____ like/different from _____?
What are the strengths and weaknesses of _____?

What are the causes of _____?
What are the effects of _____?

Can I identify any trends?
How does _____ relate to _____?
What are the potential positive/negative impacts of _____?
Who/what will _____ impact on?
What are the possible ripple effects?

Now you need to **synthesize** your information. That means you will be creating new ideas by linking them to other knowledge you have and your own personal ideas.

What are the implications of _____?
Who or what will _____ influence?
What does _____ mean to me/my family/my community/the environment...?
Does _____ really matter? Why?
How can I use _____?

What is the importance of _____?
So what?

My opinion about _____ is _____.

Now you are ready to explain, design, invent, show, demonstrate, teach...

Group Response to Text

Text/media/article/Web site_____

Student: _____

Student: _____

Common Understandings

Student: _____

Student: _____

Today You Are the Data Digger

Name: _____ Group: _____

Book: _____

Reading for today is page _____ to page _____

Data Digger: Your job is to read a section of your book and find fascinating bits of information. Jot down these gems on your organizer and record why this data is important. Prepare to share with your group.

Interesting Data	Why it Is Important

Put a star beside the most exciting data. Make sure you share this with your group.

Today You Are the Illustrator

Name:_____ Group:_____

Book: _____

Reading for today is page _____ to page _____

Illustrator: Your job is to read a section of your book and decide how you can share the information you have discovered using an illustration. It can be a picture, cartoon, labeled sketch, graph, etc. Prepare to share with your group.

Today You Are the Questioner

Name:_____ Group:_____

Book: _____

Reading for today is page _____ to page _____

Questioner: Your job is to skim through your book and read pictures, graphics, headlines and sub-titles. As you are skimming, jot down questions you have about things you are discovering. Put adhesive notes on the pages you have questions about so you can find them quickly when you are sharing with your group.

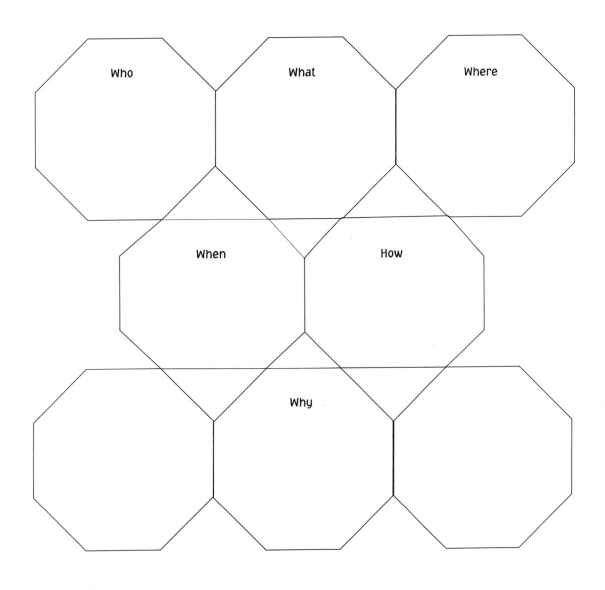

Who

What

Where

When

How

Why

Today You Are the Reflector

Name:_____ Group:_____

Book: _____

Reading for today is page _____ to page _____

Reflector: Read a section in your book. Use the reflection prompts on your organizer to help you make connections to your new discoveries. Prepare to share with your group.

A big idea I discovered is_____
_____
_____

I can use this information _____
_____
_____

I was surprised to find out that_____
_____

because _____
_____
_____

I didn't know that _____
_____
_____

I think that_____
_____

because _____
_____

The most important thing to remember is _____
_____
_____

I wonder if _____
_____
_____

Today You Are the Wordsmith

Name: _____ Group: _____

Book: _____

Reading for today is page _____ to page _____

Wordsmith: Your job is to read a section of your book. As you read, watch for new and interesting words and phrases. Record these words and phrases, as well as what you think they mean. Use a dictionary to make sure you have the correct meaning. Plan to share your words and phrases with the group.

Interesting Word/Phrase	What It Means

The word/phrase of the day is _____

Why?

Spin

name: _____

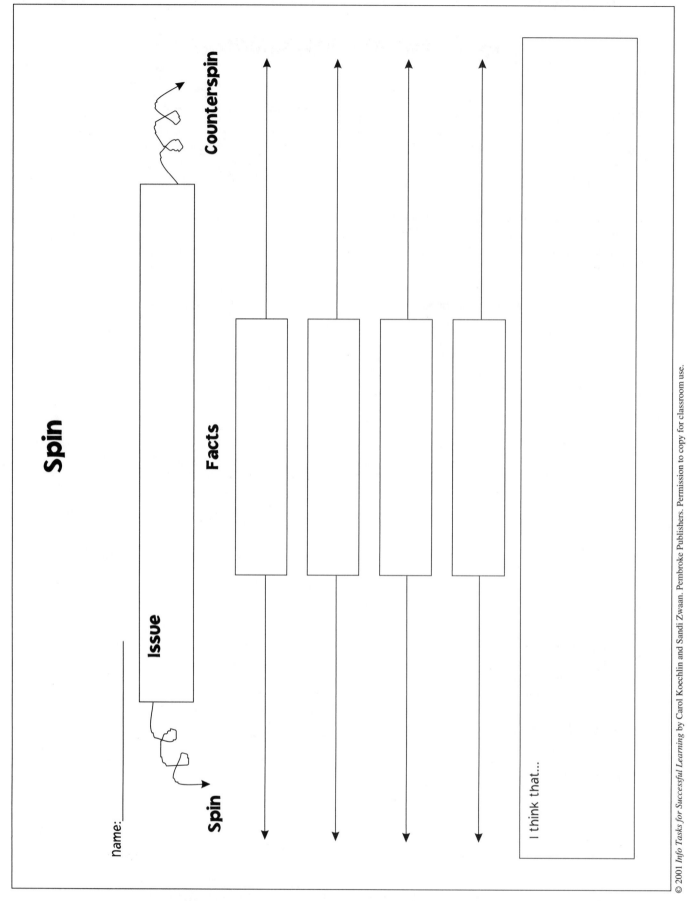

Issue

Spin

Facts

Counterspin

I think that...

Drawing Conclusions

name:_____   Inquiry question/statement:_____

My Big Ideas	Supporting Evidence

Have you examined all relevant points of view? Can you identify patterns and trends? Based on this evidence, what conclusions can you draw?

How can you use your new knowledge? What do you think is important? Why? How can you share it with others?

My Point of View

name: _____

That's Good	Why?	That's Bad	Why?
I think that…			
On the other hand…			
My personal view…			

Thinking about Understanding

Name: _____

Today I _____
_____
_____

During the process I discovered_____
_____
_____

I had some difficulty with_____
_____
_____

I found it helpful to_____
_____
_____

I thought about_____
_____
_____

Now I understand_____
_____
_____

I would still like to know_____
_____
_____

Perhaps I can_____
_____
_____

Making Judgments

name: _____

Event/Discovery	Date/Location	Significance +	−

Based on this evidence I think that...

Media Analysis

Name: _____

Technical Elements	Worth Noting
• Camera angle	
• Sound track	
• Lighting	
• Setting	
• Special effects	
•	
•	

Content Elements	Worth Noting
• Messages	
• Validity	
• Effectiveness	
•	
•	

Personal Response—quality, connections, feelings, recommendations

Pondering Perspective

Name: _____

Issue: _____

This issue is important to ___, ___, ___, ___, ___

It is important because...

I wonder
- Who...
- What...
- When...
- Where...
- How...
- Why ...
- If...

What perspectives do I need to consider?

❑ culture	❑ gender	❑ age
❑ education	❑ politics	❑ economics
❑ arts	❑ environment	❑ disability
❑ country	❑ occupation	❑ recreation

Investigating Impact

This is good news for _____ because _____

This is bad news for _____ because _____

How will this affect people? Now and in the future? Consider all concerned parties.

How will this affect the environment? Now and in the future?
Consider land, air, water, plants, animals

Who pays? Directly/Indirectly

Who gains? Directly/Indirectly

Who loses? Directly/Indirectly

What are the benefits? Why?

What are the drawbacks? Why?

Possible impact

Synthesizing—Making New Meaning

Name: _____

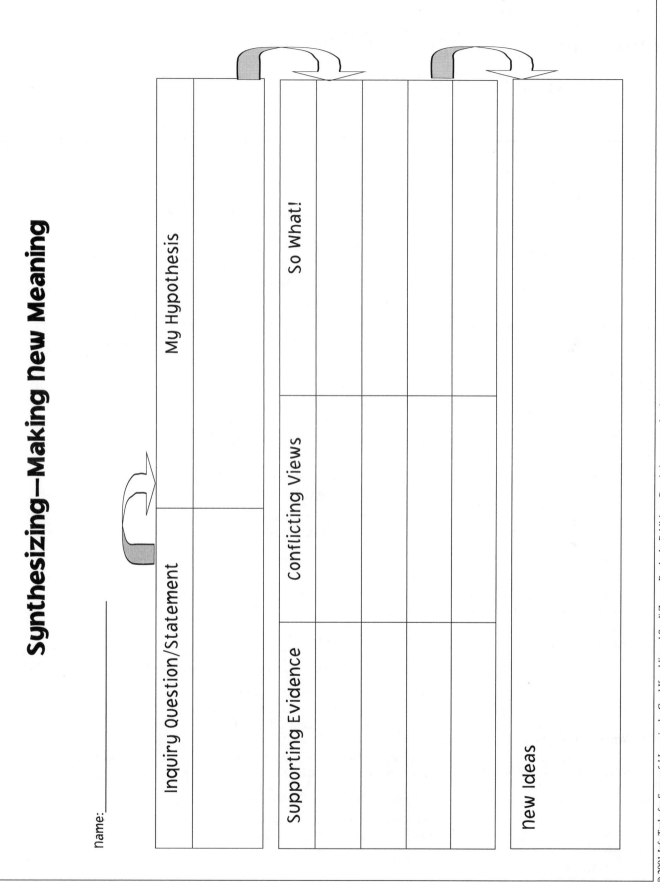

Inquiry Question/Statement	My Hypothesis

Supporting Evidence	Conflicting Views	So What!

New Ideas

Glossary of Terms for Information Tasks

Affecting — causing a change

Analyzing — separating something into its parts and thinking about or discussing the parts

Arranging — organizing items or events methodically

Bias — an attitude based on prejudice

Brainstorming — thinking about lots and lots of ideas about a specific topic

Cause and effect — a sequence of events where one thing impacts on another

Clarifying — making things or ideas understandable

Classifying — arranging things or ideas systematically based on a class or category

Clustering — looking for similarities among things or ideas, and grouping them according to characteristics

Comparing — identifying similarities among things or ideas

Concluding (conclusion n) — making a decision about

Contrasting — finding differences among things or ideas

Criteria — a standard used for judging things

Describing — communicating an impression without making a judgment

Differentiating — identifying the differences among things

Effect — the result of some action or situation

Evaluating — judging something carefully, giving both positive and negative aspects

Fact — something that is true

Generalizing (generalization n) — describing the overall picture without attention to details

Impact — a powerful effect

Inferring — coming to a conclusion by reasoning and using evidence

Interpreting — making something plain and understandable

Jigsaw — a strategy in which students in home groups learn about a topic then move to new groups where they act as experts on that topic; experts share their knowledge with each other then move back to home groups to share new learning

Judging (judgment n) — assessing, evaluating, determining the worth of something

Labeling — classifying, designating

Opinion — a carefully thought-out conclusion based on facts

Order — a systematic arrangement

Outlining — organizing the main and supporting points and ideas of a topic based on their relationships to each other

Perspective — a special point of view

Point of view — a position from which things are considered

Predicting — telling what you believe will happen in the future

Proving — using factual evidence, clear examples and logical reasons to show that a statement or situation is true

Relating — showing how situations or things are connected with one another

Scanning — looking for a specific piece of information such as a fact or phone number

Sequence — things following one another in order

Skimming — looking at the title, first paragraph or first sentence of each paragraph, as well as the illustrations and last paragraph

Sorting — arranging or separating into grades, kinds or sizes

Soundscape — sounds (e.g., vocal, instrumental, nature, etc.) that create an atmosphere or enhance a scene

Summarizing — stating the main points or facts of a subject without judging them

Synthesizing — developing personal ideas and creating something new with your learning; putting it all together to make a new form

Trends — things that are generally the same or going in the same direction

Professional Resources

Armstrong, Tricia. 2000. *Information Transformation: Teaching Strategies for Authentic Research, Projects and Activities.* Markham, ON: Pembroke.

Bromely, Karen. 1995. *Graphic Organizers: Visual Strategies for Active Learning.* Toronto, ON: Scholastic.

Daniels, Harvey. 1994. *Literature Circles.* Portland, ME: Stenhouse.

Davies, Anne, Caren Cameron, Colleen Politano and Kathleen Gregory. 1992. *Together Is Better: Collaborative Assessment, Evaluation & Reporting.* Winnipeg, MB: Peguis.

Galbraith, McClelland et al. 1996. *Analyzing Issues: Science, Technology & Society.* Toronto, ON: Trifolium Books.

Gardner, Howard. 1993. *Multiple Intelligences: The Theory in Practice.* New York: HarperCollins.

Gregory, Kathleen, Caren Cameron and Anne Davies. 1997. *Setting and Using Criteria.* Winnipeg, MB: Peguis.

Harvey, Stephanie. 1998. *Nonfiction Matters: Reading, Writing and Research in Grades 3-8.* Portland, ME: Stenhouse.

Harvey, Stephanie and Anne Goudvis. 2000. *Strategies That Work.* Portland, ME: Stenhouse.

Hyerle, David. 1996. *Visual Tools for Constructing Knowledge.* Alexandria, VA: Association for Supervision and Curriculum Development.

Koechlin, Carol and Sandi Zwaan. 1997. *Teaching Tools for the Information Age.* Markham, ON: Pembroke.

Koechlin, Carol and Sandi Zwaan. 1997. *Information Power Pack Intermediate Skillsbook.* Markham, ON: Pembroke.

Koechlin, Carol and Sandi Zwaan. 1997. *Information Power Pack Junior Skillsbook.* Markham, ON: Pembroke.

Moline, Steve. 1995. *I See What You Mean: Children at Work with Visual Information K-8.* Portland, ME: Stenhouse.

Morgan, Nora and Juliana Saxton. 1994. *Asking Better Questions: Models, Techniques and Classroom Activities for Engaging Students in Learning.* Markham, ON: Pembroke.

Parry, Terence and Gayle Gregory. 1998. *Designing Brain Compatible Learning.* Arlington Heights: Skylight.

Schwartz, Linda and Kathlene Willing. 2001. *Computer Activities for the Cooperative Classroom.* Markham, ON: Pembroke.

Wilhelm, Jeffery D. and Paul Freidemann, with Julie Erickson. 1998. *Hyperlearning: Where Projects, Inquiry, and Research Meet.* Portland, ME: Stenhouse.

Wiggins & McTighe. 1999. *Understanding by Design.* Alexandria VA: Association for Supervision and Curriculum Development.

Web sites

American Association of School Librarians
http://www.ala.org/aasl/

Debbie Abilock Curriculum Site
http://nueveaschool.org/~debbie/library/overview.html

From Now On—The Educational Technology, by Jamie McKenzie
http://www.fno.org

The Graphic Organizer
http://www.graphic.org/

Jigsaw Classroom
http://www.jigsaw.org/

Kathy Schrock's Guide for Educators
http://school.discovery.com/schrockguide/index.html

Media Awareness Network
http://www.media-awareness.ca/

Ontario School Library Association
http://www.accessola.org/action/positions/info_studies/

The WebQuest Page
http://edweb.sdsu.edu/webquest/webquest.html

http://school.discovery.com/schoolhome.html

Index

Note: Page numbers in italic indicate reproducible pages.